IMAGES
*of America*

# RUTHERFORD COUNTY IN WORLD WAR II

*Each veteran and each supporter of the country during World War II has his or her own memories. Below are some of the "idle memories" from Harold Stallcup, Station 131, Nuthampstead, England, 601st Squadron, 398th Bomb Group. Many of these thoughts are unique to Stallcup's situation, but others are typical of service personnel everywhere.*

## IDLE MEMORIES OF SIGHTS, SOUNDS, AND SENSATIONS FROM STATION 131, NUTHAMPSTEAD, ENGLAND

Harold K. Stallcup

Squadron 601, 398 B.G.

- Mail Call! The joy of mail from home and the disappointment when there was none.
- Real eggs for breakfast on mission days.
- The Chaplain, quiet, concerned, and available before missions.
- The hushed voices and tensions before briefing begins.
- The involuntary and barely audible reactions when the curtain is pulled revealing the target for the day.
- Meeting your crew at the airplane. Trying to be reassuring and businesslike at the same time.
- A visit and concert by Glen Miller orchestra.
- The quiet resolve of the English people during all their suffering and tribulations.
- "Flak Leave"-several days away from the war, but it is still on your mind and you are still a long way from home.
- Freezing weather and dense fog for several days at a time, making the landscape a winter wonderland.
- Trying to stay warm in a Nissen hut with coal rationed.
- The German counteroffensive in Belgium, December of 1944. We were grounded by weather when we were so desperately needed by our troops.
- Christmas Eve, 1944. A break in the weather! An all-out mission with every available plane and crew to fly. This broke the back of the German counteroffensive.
- Finishing my missions, January, 1945.
- Anticipating going home and seeing my family including my twin sons who were born while I was at Nuthampstead.
- Saying goodbye to my friends and crew members who were not yet finished with their missions.

The thoughts of others in the air, on the sea, on the land, and in combat may vary slightly from the thoughts above, but the consensus would have been the same: "Our country's at war, and we all must help it be won." Our thanks to all who did their part to ensure the freedoms we all hold dear.

*(on the cover)* The chaplain of the USS *Biloxi* conducts worship services on the quarterdeck in 1945. The lifebelts on the sailors and the slender barrels of the six-inch guns are reminders that the war is raging even at this peaceful occasion. The photograph is courtesy of Dwight ("Buck") Green.

IMAGES
*of America*

# RUTHERFORD COUNTY IN WORLD WAR II

Anita Price Davis and James M. Walker

ARCADIA
PUBLISHING

ISBN 978-0-7385-1426-7

Published by Arcadia Publishing
Charleston, South Carolina

Printed in the United States of America

Library of Congress Catalog Card Number: 2003103772

For all general information contact Arcadia Publishing at:
Telephone 843-853-2070
Fax 843-853-0044
E-mail sales@arcadiapublishing.com
For customer service and orders:
Toll-Free 1-888-313-2665

Visit us on the Internet at www.arcadiapublishing.com

*In memory of Jim's parents,*
*Nelle Culbreth Walker and James Maze Walker,*
*and Anita's parents,*
*Nellie Daves Price Burns and Arthur Fred Price.*

# FOREWORD

Our book begins with an apology. It was impossible to include each person in Rutherford County who was in service or who contributed on the homefront to World War II. Consider these facts: About 5,000 people from Rutherford County were in service during World War II; about 42,000 people remained in the county. Each was essential to the war effort. The fact that we did not include each of them is not to diminish personal sacrifice and contribution. It was just impossible to include everyone. We begin this volume, therefore, with the regret that we could not incorporate all.

# CONTENTS

# ACKNOWLEDGMENTS

This book is not the work of one person. Many people deserve credit. On each photograph or illustration we have tried to identify the specific source. There are some contributors, however, who have been instrumental in the completion of this work. Special thanks go to Edith Owens. We used many, many sources, particularly the works of Clarence Griffin and the armed services. We are grateful to Rutherford County and Converse College (which has encouraged this project of ours); Alice Bradley, Billy Seay, Jean Gordon, Mike Pyle, Ken Morrow, Sarah Daves, Jim Brown, the *Daily Courier*, Jim Bishop, WCAB, the Senior Citizen Center, Bethel Baptist Church of Ellenboro, Duke Power Company, the American Legion, the Veterans of Foreign Wars and VFW Auxiliary, First Baptist Church of Forest City, Alexander Baptist Church, Kiwanis Club, Chimney Rock Baptist Church, relatives and friends of the veterans, Mae Blanton, and, most importantly, the veterans themselves to whom we all owe so much. The photograph below is of Harold K. Stallcup, the author of "Idle Memories" (page 2); the photograph is courtesy of him.

# INTRODUCTION

The 1930s brought economic hardship to the nation and to the world. War had already begun abroad and was beginning to spread from nation to nation like an uncontrolled forest fire. On Sunday, December 7, 1941, the flames seared the United States. The Japanese attack on Pearl Harbor rocked the nation. The following day, President Franklin D. Roosevelt predicted that December 7th "would live in infamy." After his speech, Congress formally declared war against the Empire of Japan. This conflict added to the already raging World War II.

World War II "hit Rutherford County like a great blight." (Clarence Griffin, *History of Rutherford County, 1937–1951*, p. 18) The population of the county at that time was approximately 42,000. More than 5,000 men from the county took part in the war; this number was more than 12 percent of the county's total population. Because the state of North Carolina had 361,000 people who served in the military and because there were 100 counties in the state, the county sacrificially gave more than its share of enlisted men.

North Carolina had 4,088 who died in service; this was more than three percent of the total number of men from the United States who died in World War II. Based on the number of counties and the number from the state who died in service, the number of men sacrificed from Rutherford County statistically should have been no more than 41. Instead, Rutherford County lost 148 fine young men; this was more than 3.5 times its "fair" share.

> Nothing else had ever approached these figures, except in the days of the Civil War when about sixteen percent of the population was engaged in the conflict, which led one Confederate official to remark that the seed corn of the South was being used in that conflict. Of the 21 counties of western North Carolina, Rutherford had furnished the second largest number of men. . .excelled only by Buncombe [a county with three times the population of Rutherford County]. (Griffin, pp. 18–19.)

The average age of the Rutherford County man who died serving his country during World War II was 24 years. The youngest was 18; the oldest was 42. More than 36 percent of those killed from the county were married. One of these married men had four children; another had three. A total of 34 children in Rutherford County lost their fathers during World War II.

Rutherford County citizens began their sacrifice on the day of the Japanese attack on Pearl Harbor. Mark Alexander Rhodes, Seaman, United States Navy, of the Providence community of Forest City, Route 1, was the first man from the county to make the supreme sacrifice. Seaman Rhodes was killed in action when the ill-fated USS *Arizona* was sunk. (*Forest City Courier*, August 12, 1945.)

Throughout and after World War II, the Rutherford County military men continued to give their best. World War II ended in 1945 when Germany surrendered on May 8 and when Japan capitulated on August 14. Rutherford County men in the military had to complete tours of duty and endure continued exposure to illness and danger. Four additional men from Rutherford County died in military service after August 14 but before the end of 1945.

Those remaining in Rutherford County had to endure hardships also. Scarcely a home in Rutherford County was not affected in some manner by the selective service. The sentiment was almost unanimous that the war must be won. Those at home were determined to do their part to bring the boys back home. Women entered industry to take the place of men who had gone to war. A manpower shortage developed; this scarcity required not only the women but also the older residents in retirement to enter again the list of workers. All of Rutherford County's textile plants were producing war goods and operating on full schedule. This called for many additional workers. Then President Roosevelt appealed to the American people saying that America must be the arsenal of democracy.

> The manpower shortage was keenly felt on the farms. The farmers were called upon to increase both their acreage and production per acre. This they managed to do, in face

of the fact that increased production was attained with less help than in the days when production was much lower.

With about one-fourth of the country's available manpower in service, the citizens at home had to shoulder the additional load and double production, in mills, on farms, with two men instead of eight.

But long hours of production were not the entire story. Many of these workers were connected with the various branches of the Office of Civilian Defense, which took up what little leisure time they had. (Griffin, p. 19.)

What was the attitude of those remaining in Rutherford County? Rutherford County mothers and fathers never forgot the child who was away; wives continued to grieve absent husbands; children missed their fathers. Religious faith helped many at home and abroad to endure. Most churches in Rutherford County were open for daily prayer.

The ringing of the church bells at noon each day is the call to prayer . . . Any and all citizens are urged to share in these seasons of prayer. At that time one of the churches is open for any who will deny themselves a few minutes to come and join in the privileges of prayer. Any and all citizens are urged to share in these seasons of united prayer for our churches, our nation, our world, our fellow-citizens in the armed forces, and the coming of the King of Peace. If you care, come to the church for prayer. But wherever you are, take a few minutes immediately following the ringing of the bells for earnest, fervent prayer. (*Rutherford County News*, May 11, 1944.)

Blue stars hung in the windows to mark the absence of a family member in service. Many of these stars changed to gold as telegrams and letters arrived announcing the loss of the loved one. Three Rutherford County families received two such notices; the Ruppe, McKinney, and Hall families sadly but proudly changed two blue stars in their windows to gold ones. Their six "real heroes" were Lynn T. (September 23, 1943) and Toy Ruppe (September 13, 1944); Daniel K. (January 25, 1945) and Gilkey A. Hall Jr. (June 7, 1944); and Broadus H. (December 11, 1944) and R. Earl McKinney (September 22, 1944). Tri-High School sacrificed also. Seventeen young men from Tri-High School, which served Avondale, Henrietta, and Caroleen, died in service of their country.

All those who served and all those left behind sacrificed also. Citizens from Rutherford County entered all branches of service: the Army, the Navy, the Marines, and the Army Air Forces. They served as paratroopers, fighter pilots, riflemen, waist gunners, medics, infantrymen, seamen, and engineers, to name a few roles. They performed their appointed tasks, big and small, as they had been taught: well. Not only did they respond to the challenge, they excelled in their service to their country and distinguished themselves. Those in command bestowed upon the county's personnel many awards, some posthumously. These awards included the Bronze Star, the Silver Star, the Air Medal, the Good Conduct Medal, and the Combat Infantryman's Badge. One Rutherford County man received the soldier's medal for demonstrated heroism not involving actual conflict with an enemy at personal hazard or danger and at the voluntary risk of life under conditions not involving conflict with an armed enemy. When a fire broke out in the barracks in Occupied Japan, Pvt. John O. Brackett could have escaped but he remained to help the other men to escape. His actions "reflected the utmost credit upon himself and the military service." Some county men received the Purple Heart. From 1932 until September 1942, this award was for merit and for war wounds; thereafter, the award went only to those classified as KIA (killed in action), WIA (wounded in action), or DOW (died of wounds). Even those without these most distinguished awards gave to their country. These many awards were fitting, deserved, and appreciated. But we, too, can bestow upon those who served an important gift: we can listen and we can remember.

The purpose of these pages is to allow Rutherford County people to tell the story of World War II through their eyes. We who remain must remember; this book will help us to do so. Faces and facts are fast fading. This book will become a lasting record: *Rutherford County in World War II*.

# *One*

# Pearl Harbor (1941)
## Rutherford County Enters the War

*On December 7, 1941, 200 Japanese aircraft suddenly attacked the American fleet at Pearl Harbor and nearby Navy and Army bases. The attack sank the USS* Arizona; *seven more vessels received severe damage. Japan attacked without a declaration of war. At the same time, Japan struck at Hong Kong, Thailand, the Malay States, and the Philippines.*

This photograph on December 7, 1941, shows the USS *Arizona* (BB-39) burning furiously and listing after the surprise attack. The photograph is courtesy of the United States Navy.

Mark Alexander Rhodes, Seaman, United States Navy, of the Providence community, Forest City, Route 1, was the first casualty of Rutherford County. Seaman Rhodes was killed in action when the ill-fated USS *Arizona* (BB-39) sank at Pearl Harbor. From left to right are Mary Rhodes, Mark Rhodes, and Lorene Padgett Hopson. (Courtesy of Lorene Padgett Hopson.)

Edgar Green, of the United States Navy and a Rutherford County native, entered the service in 1938. His assignment was to Pearl Harbor and the battleship *Oklahoma*. Green, however, was on detached duty when the attack occurred. As a result of the attack, the *Oklahoma* capsized; Green's detachment at the time may have saved his life. The photograph is courtesy of the United States Navy.

"On December 7, 1941, I was in the 14th Naval District Headquarters crew of Adm. C.C. Bloch," Edgar Green recalls. Green remembers the ringing phone of that morning and the excited voice telling him "the Japanese are attacking!" Green shouted into the receiver, "You're drunk! Go back to bed!" Then he, too, heard the commotion. When Edgar ran outside, he saw one plane so low, "I could see the teeth of the pilot. I immediately drew my .45 and began shooting at the plane. We set up a first-aid station on the pier at Ford Island where we would take the people we picked out of the water. I worked from Sunday at 7:00 a.m. until Wednesday at 4:00 a.m. rescuing survivors and helping the injured and dying. I ate one bologna sandwich during the entire 69-hour period." (Courtesy of the United States Navy.)

Edgar Green (on the left) retired from the Navy after serving for 22 years. His duty during World War II included both Pearl Harbor and Midway; in 2003 he had a residence in Florida, as well as Ellenboro. Edgar's brother (on the right) was Dwight ("Buck") Green who served aboard the light cruiser USS *Biloxi*. Dwight died shortly after his interview in January 2003. (Courtesy of Edgar Green and Dwight Green.)

June Wright is the ninth from the left in the front row of this photograph of the Headquarters Battery, 11th Field Artillery, Schofield Barracks. June and the other men pictured were all at Pearl Harbor on December 7, 1941. After June's discharge in 1944, he re-enlisted and served a total of 22 years. (Courtesy of June Wright and the United States Army.)

During the Japanese attack on Pearl Harbor, the 24th Infantry Division received credit for shooting down five of the attacking planes. This photograph shows a Japanese Zero shot down during the attack. (Courtesy of the United States Navy.)

An Act of Congress (1990) approved the issue of a commemorative medallion to survivors of the attack on Pearl Harbor. This medallion belongs to June Wright, 11th Field Artillery. Wright, who now resides in Rutherford County, was present at Pearl Harbor on December 7, 1941. He received the medallion in appreciation of his service. (Courtesy of June Wright.)

The reverse of the medallion indicates "For Those Who Served." Congress awarded the medallion to June Wright. (Courtesy of June Wright.)

This photograph shows the USS *Cassin* and the USS *Downes* after the attack on Pearl Harbor. This December defeat of the United States prompted outrage from all levels of the American population; a total of 18 warships were sunk or heavily damaged. Two battleships were total losses, including the *Oklahoma* and the *Arizona*; 200 aircraft were destroyed; and 2,400 soldiers, sailors, and Marines were killed. By contrast, Japan lost 50 men, 28 aircraft, and 5 midget submarines. On December 8, 1941, President Franklin D. Roosevelt declared that December 7 would be "a day that would live in infamy." After his speech Congress declared war against the Empire of Japan. (Courtesy of the United States Navy.)

Pearl Harbor, Oahu Island, was home port for the Navy's Pacific fleet. (Courtesy of James M. Walker.)

# *Two*

# Doolittle's Raid, Coral Sea, and Midway (1942)

## Impeding the Japanese

*The "Coral Sea" and "Midway" were locations that most Americans in the 1940s had to research; their geography lessons had not prepared them to identify these places in the news without the aid of an atlas, globe, or map. Many young American servicemen found themselves transferred to places that they never before knew existed. Many families began to mark the travels of their loved ones with flags on a world map, if the information was not "classified."*

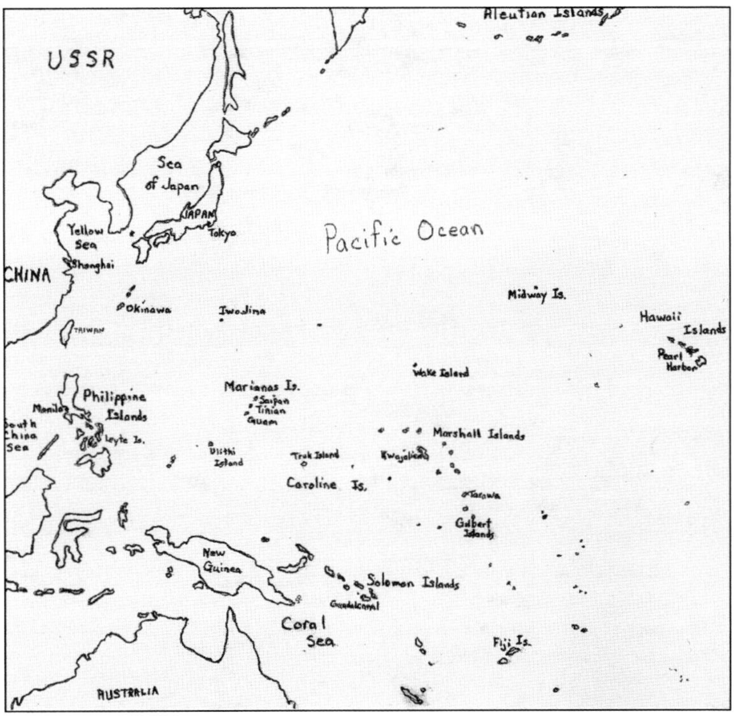


For five months after the attack on Pearl Harbor (December 7, 1941), Japan advanced into the Southwest Pacific. The Battle of the Coral Sea (May 7–8, 1942) stopped this expansion. The Battle of Midway (June 3–7, 1942) ended the Empire's drive in the Central Pacific. (Courtesy of James M. Walker.)

Fred O. Morgan's ship, the USS *Hornet*, took part in the famous Doolittle Raid on Tokyo on April 18, 1942. The *Hornet* launched 16 B-25 Army bombers against Tokyo and other targets. The raid was a huge morale booster to United States forces. (Courtesy of the United States Navy.)

The United States suffered the major loss of the aircraft carrier USS *Lexington* on May 8, 1942—the second day of the Battle of the Coral Sea—but was able to claim a strategic victory. The 33,000-ton aircraft carrier waged its fight, first against attacking Japanese planes, and second against a series of internal explosions. During the eruptions, Adm. Aubrey Fitch directed Capt. F.C. Sherman to abandon ship. When the carrier did not sink of its own accord, the destroyer *Phelps* delivered five torpedoes that sank the *Lexington* at 19:32. About 90 percent of the crew of 3,000 survived the ordeal. (Courtesy of the United States Navy.)

Tiny Midway Island was an important outpost for patrol planes based there and for refueling submarines headed west to Japan. The most populous inhabitants of Midway Island were the gooney birds. The birds often lined Midway's shores; even during some of the fiercest fighting on the islands, they usually appeared undisturbed by all the activity and noise. (Courtesy of A.C. Spratt Jr. of Ellenboro, North Carolina.)

For the servicemen on Midway, a chapel could provide the solace needed for the long days ahead. This Quonset hut devoted to worship was important to many of the servicemen stationed on the island. (Courtesy of A.C. Spratt Jr.)

Through code breaking, the Navy learned of the ominous Japanese attack planned for Midway Island. Adm. Chester Nimitz, Commander in Chief of the Pacific Fleet, ordered three aircraft carriers (with supporting cruisers and destroyers) to lie in wait northeast of Midway and to attack when American patrol planes spotted the enemy. This photograph shows SBD Dauntless dive bombers from Task Force 16 as they make a bombing run on a burning Japanese ship (right center). (Courtesy of the United States Navy.)

Rutherford County natives Fred O. Morgan and his brother Worth G. Morgan were present at the great confrontation at Midway. Machinist Mate 1/c Fred Morgan was aboard the carrier USS *Hornet*. Aboard the USS *Vincennes*, a heavy cruiser, was his brother Machinist Mate Worth G. Morgan. The *Hornet* has planes spotted on her flight deck; the *Vincennes* is astern. In the foreground is the USS *Atlanta*, an anti-aircraft cruiser christened by Margaret Mitchell; Japanese gunfire sank the cruiser on November 13, 1942, off Guadalcanal. (Courtesy of the United States Navy.)

The five-day (June 3–7, 1942) confrontation that followed was the Battle of Midway. Edgar Green, Rutherford County native, witnessed the fierce struggle and mourned the loss of many brave American servicemen. He was stationed on Midway for nine months. The losses of the United States Navy included one aircraft carrier (the *Yorktown*) and one destroyer (*Hammon*). The scene above shows the *Yorktown* on June 3, 1942. The Japanese fleet suffered the loss of four aircraft carriers and their irreplaceable pilots. (Courtesy of the United States Navy.)

Japanese aircraft from four carriers struck Midway Island in early morning of June 3, 1942. This view shows some of the damage caused by the Japanese. (Courtesy of the United States Navy.)

Midway Island found out on June 3, 1942 that it was to be the target of Japanese attacks from the air. Even though the oil storage tanks are burning furiously, the gooney birds in the foreground seem unaffected by the conflagration. (Courtesy of the United States Navy.)

A.C. Spratt Jr. (left) was drafted into the Marine Corps on March 24, 1942. Assigned to the 6th Defense Battalion, here he appears with Emil Quinn (right) in Hawaii before they left for Midway Island. (Courtesy of A.C. Spratt Jr.)

Midway was used as an advanced base to top off fuel for units of the fleet. This 1944 photograph shows an escort carrier and a docked destroyer escort; a F4U Corsair fighter sits on the pier. (Courtesy of A.C. Spratt Jr.)

Pacific Islanders used large glass floats on their fishing nets; this one was about the size of a basketball. A.C. Spratt Jr. was a member of the 6th Marine Defense Battalion, which defended Midway Island from 1944 through 1945. He brought this float and several smaller glass floats back to Rutherford County with him. (Courtesy of A.C. Spratt Jr.)

After the Battle of Midway, the Marine Corps 6th Defense Battalion defended the island until the end of World War II. This 105-mm howitzer was part of the island's defense. (Courtesy of A.C. Spratt Jr.)

A.C. Spratt Jr. served in the United States Marine Corps from March 24, 1944, until his discharge on January 21, 1946. (Courtesy of A.C. Spratt Jr.)

# *Three*

# The Air Offensive of Europe (1942–1945)

## Bringing the War to Hitler

*In July 1942, the Army Air Forces started daylight bombing raids over occupied France. From bases in England, squadrons of the Eighth Air Force dropped their bombs on railways, factories, and troop concentrations. These raids continued until May 1945, the end of the war in Europe.*

This B-26 is dropping a string of 100-pound bombs on occupied France. Mike Davis helped to photograph the results of these raids for the United States. (Courtesy of the Army Air Forces.)

Sgt. Mike Davis of the 19th Photo Tech developed aerial reconnaissance photographs of bomb damage. This photograph shows the crater field left by an Air Force raid on occupied France. Analysis of these photographs allowed commanding officers to determine which targets had been successfully attached. (Courtesy of Mike Davis.)

The crew of the B-24 "Dixie Jewel" admires the nose art of their plane. The motto "Hard to Get" was unfortunately not true. On February 21, 1944, the "Dixie Jewel" was shot down over Muenster, Germany. (Courtesy of Guy T. Padgett.)

Technical Sgt. Guy T. Padgett was the radio operator on the "Dixie Jewel" (a B-24 bomber of the 714th squad/44th Bomb Group/8th Air Force) out of Seething Air Force Base, Norfolk, England. Padgett had to parachute from 23,000 feet when his plane was shot down. Padgett said that his "parachute opened with the sound of a bomb. It was a good sound." (Courtesy of Guy T. Padgett.)

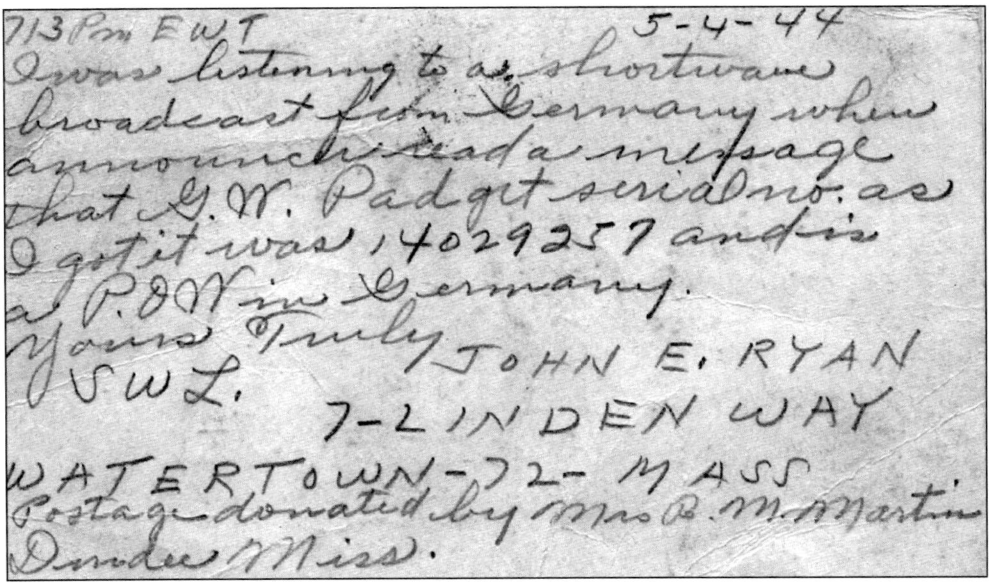

713 Pm EWT 5-4-44
I was listening to a shortwave broadcast from Germany when announcer read a message that G.W. Padgett serial no. as I got it was 14029257 and is a P.O.W. in Germany.
Yours Truly JOHN E. RYAN
SWL.
7-LINDEN WAY
WATERTOWN-72- MASS
Postage donated by Mrs P.M. Martin Dundee Miss.

Guy T. Padgett's parents received this postcard from a stranger (John E. Ryan in Watertown, Massachusetts). Ryan heard on the short wave radio a broadcast from Germany that Guy Padgett was a prisoner of war (POW) there. The postmark for the card indicated a mailing date of May 4, 1944; the postage came from Mrs. P.M. Martin in Dundee, Mississippi. (Courtesy of Guy T. Padgett.)

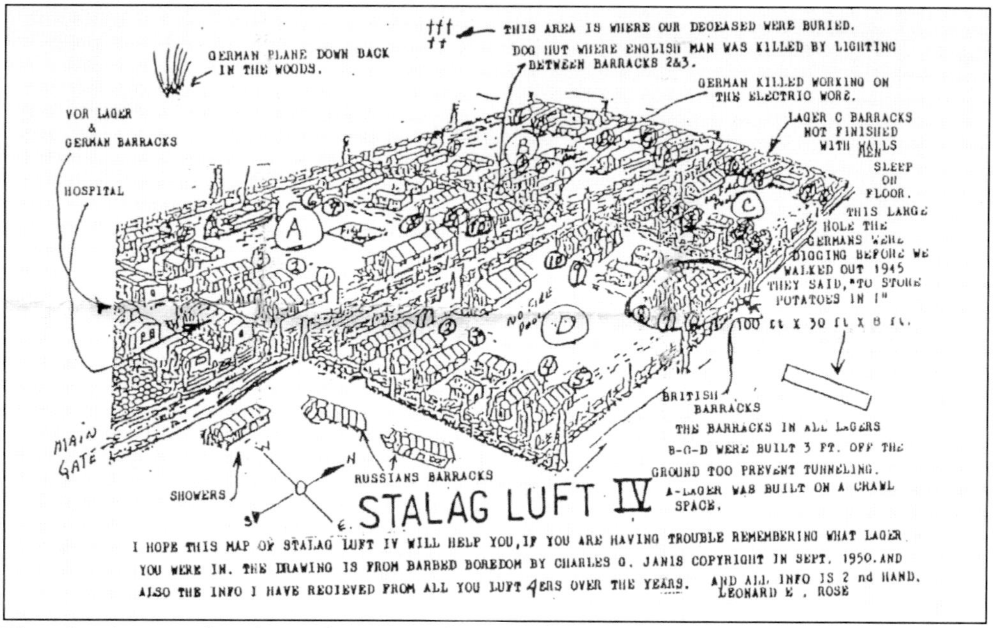


This sketch-map of Stalag Luft IV in Lithuania shows the "home" of approximately 10,000 Allied enlisted men who were prisoners of war. Among these was Guy T. Padgett and James Settlemeyer from the county. (Courtesy of Leonard E. Rose [publisher of *Barbed Boredom*] and Guy T. Padgett.)

Blaine Logan's assignment was to the Aircraft Parts Supply at Wharton Air Force Base, England. At Wharton, fighters and bombers were made ready for combat. The bombers were air ferried from the United States, and the fighters were convoyed to Liverpool. The aircraft were sent to various bases in Southern England. Logan, a member of the 8th Air Force, appears here in uniform in Wharton, England. (Courtesy of Blaine B. Logan Jr.)

In July of 1943 Leon McDaniel was one of many servicemen who sailed to Glasgow, Scotland, on large passenger ships, like the *Aquatania*. The Cunard Liner weighed almost 46,000 tons and could carry over 10,000 soldiers per crossing. The photograph above in English waters shows the fog surrounding the ship. (Courtesy of Leon McDaniel.)

Tech-4 Leon McDaniel was in Huntingdon, England, from 1943 to 1946 with the 480th Engineer Maintenance Company. His duties included inspecting, repairing, and testing construction equipment (such as bulldozers, road graders, and power shovels) in the mobile repair shops. Here McDaniel appears in uniform during his stay in Huntingdon. (Courtesy of Leon McDaniel.)

Leon McDaniel, 480th Engineer Maintenance Company, worked with large equipment, such as this crane. McDaniel loaded and unloaded cargo for the troops in England. This large crane was typical of the heavy equipment used to construct air bases in England for the 8th Air Force. (Courtesy of Leon McDaniel.)

Divine worship services were very much a part of the life of many service personnel. These chapel services in Huntingdon, England, are in a Quonset hut. (Courtesy of Leon McDaniel.)

This is the scene of the farewell party for the 480th Engineer Maintenance Company at Huntingdon, England, in 1945. The rumor was that the unit would be going to the Pacific Theater for the final defeat of Japan. Fortunately the war ended, and the unit did not have to go. (Courtesy of Leon McDaniel.)

Harold K. Stallcup, Second Lieutenant, United States Army Air Forces, volunteered in July 1942. He trained with his crew on a B-17 named "Stud Hoss." Harold Stallcup is in the front row and is the first man kneeling on left. (Courtesy of Harold K. Stallcup.)

Harold K. Stallcup flew 30 combat missions over occupied Europe; he was a pilot of a B-17G with the 601st Squadron/398th Bomb Group/8th Air Force. After being hit on the second and fourth mission by German flak that did not explode, his radio operator Sergeant Loveless stated emphatically, "I want to fly with Captain Stallcup. The Lord flies with him." Stallcup's plane did not suffer any casualties in 30 missions. (Courtesy of Harold K. Stallcup.)

Stallcup's base was Air Station 131 near Nuthampstead, England. Stallcup's squadron participated in major raids over France and Germany. This photograph shows the Control Tower of Station 131. (Courtesy of Harold K. Stallcup.)

This B-17G of the 601st/398 Bomb Group shows the damaged inflicted by Nazi flak guns on a raid over Germany. Miraculously, only the bombardier died; the skill of Pilot Phil Stahlman and his crew brought the plane home to England. (Courtesy of Harold K. Stallcup.)

In November 1944 a wire arrived for Harold Stallcup saying, "Son born, keep smiling, son born." Stallcup had no idea that he was going to be a father of twins! Wires sent to military personnel overseas had to have the words selected from certain "stock" lines. His wife Nancy Blanton Stallcup had to be creative in her telegram. After 30 successful missions of 236 hours and 45 minutes in the cockpit, Stallcup was rotated home so that he could see his sons Larry and Steve for the first time—five months after they were born. (Courtesy of Harold K. Stallcup.)

First Lt. Robert Watkins flew a P-51 Mustang with the 358th Fighter Squadron/355th Fighter Group/Eighth Air Force based at Steeple Mordan near Cambridge, England. From 1942 until 1945 he flew 60 missions over occupied Europe in his plane named "Kitten." Watkins was credited with one possible kill and three damaged enemy aircraft. (Courtesy of Robert Watkins.)

Lt. James E. Settlemeyer, 8th Air Force, was stationed in England. As a navigator on a B-17, he engaged in the daylight raids (often targeting ball bearing factories) over occupied Europe. In late May 1944, Settlemeyer's plane was shot down over Austria. Settlemeyer parachuted out, landed in the top of a tree, and was captured and strip-searched. Hester Ann McKeithan Settlemeyer (his mother) received the telegram on her birthday, June 6, 1944. Mae remembers her mother saying, "It was the saddest birthday present I ever received." "A death pall settled over the house," Mae said. He was released by the Russians after the end of the war, was able to make his way unaided to American lines, returned to America, and completed two weeks in a hospital. (Courtesy of Mae Blanton.)

Uree native Claude R. Nelon volunteered in May 1942 for the United States Army Air Corps and was trained as a bomber pilot. From late 1944 until 1945 First Lieutenant Nelon flew nine combat missions with the 334th Bomber Squadron/95th Bomber Group/8th Air Force; they attacked targets in Berlin and Oranienburg, field storage areas near Essen, and the Ruhr industrial area of Germany. Nelon is pictured with his B-17 "Better Duck" crew at Horham, England, near Cambridge. Nelon is the second from the left in the back row. (Courtesy of Claude R. Nelon.)

Claude Nelon retired as Colonel after 31 years and nine months of service, during which he piloted B-17s, B-29s, B-36s, and B-52s. He was Aerospace Professor at Syracuse University, headed the Air Force ROTC program, and helped the university establish a Russian language program for military personnel. During his second tour of duty at his alma mater, the first female United States Air Force cadet joined the program. (Courtesy of Claude R. Nelon.)

Technical Sgt. Forrest S. Clark was a radioman-gunner on a B-24 of the 44th Bomb Group, 8th Air Force, stationed at AAF 115, Shipdham, England. The insignia for the 44th Bomb Group was a flying eight-ball. Clark's plane suffered battle damage on a bombing mission over Lechfeld, Germany, on April 13, 1944. Clark was interned in Switzerland. He escaped with the help of the French underground and passed the French border in December 1944. (Courtesy of Forrest S. Clark.)

By March 1945 Forrest Clark had been repatriated to the United States and had received orders to the Lake Lure Inn, a rest and rehabilitation center at Lake Lure, North Carolina. Clark said, "The value of the Lake Lure Rest and Rehabilitation Center was that it reaffirmed faith for many battle-shocked combat veterans. We had religious services that reinforced our spiritual faith as well as prepared us for re-entry to civilian life, marriage, and careers. There is no doubt in my mind and spirit that it had a lifelong effect on me. I think there is an important unwritten story here about the part of Lake Lure in World War II. I learned to pray in the service, and I learned the value of a spiritual dimension to my life." (Courtesy of Asheville Post Card Company, Asheville, North Carolina.)

# Four

# Guadalcanal and the Solomon Islands (1942)

## Fighting Back

*Through code breaking and photographic intelligence, the United States became aware of Japan's intentions and their work to construct an airfield in the little-developed area of Guadalcanal in the Solomon Islands. The United States immediately devised a plan to invade the area before the Japanese could complete the airfield.*

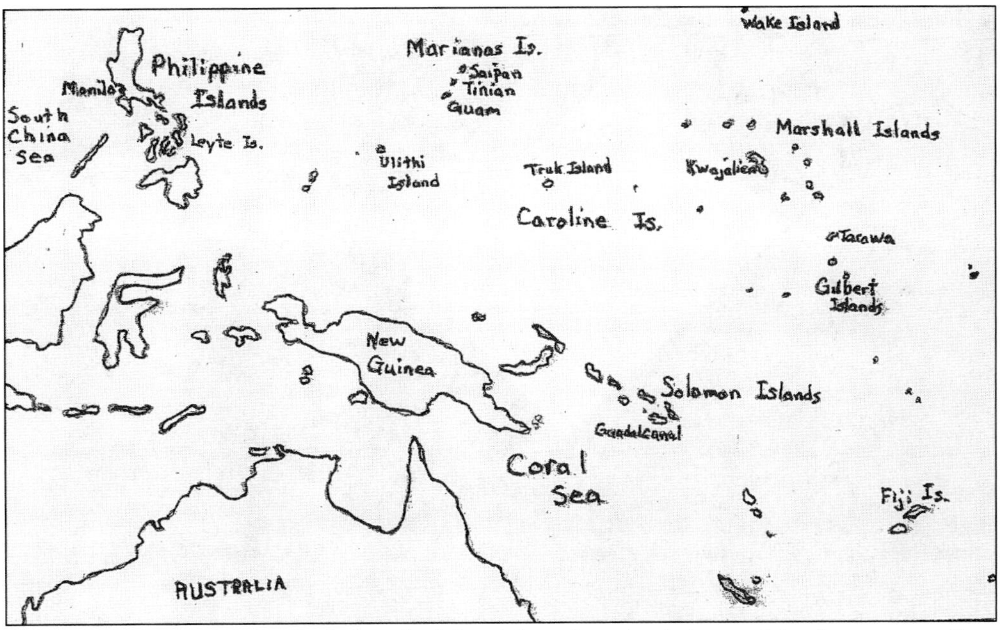


In early 1942 the Japanese had identified Guadalcanal in the Solomon Islands as an excellent airfield location. From here they could hopefully disrupt supplies and communication among Australia and the United States. (Courtesy of James M. Walker.)

On August 7, 1942, the First U.S. Marine Division made a virtually unopposed landing on Guadalcanal, a remote island in the Southwest Pacific. The invasion was just the beginning of the struggle as each side tried to obtain full control of the area. American troops would battle heat, rain, disease, hunger, and life-or-death engagements with the Japanese for six months in this little-known place. (Courtesy of United States Marine Corps.)

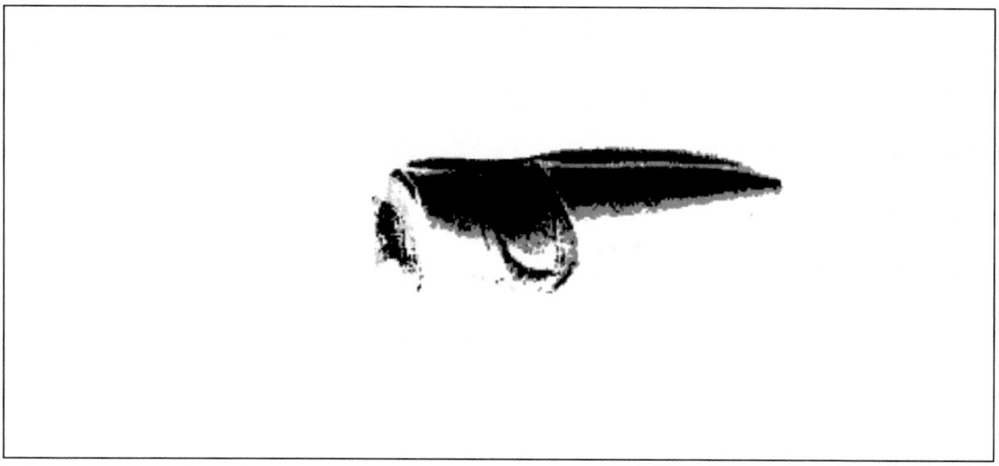

While the First U.S. Marine Division was invading Guadalcanal, the First Marine Raider Battalion was invading nearby Tulagi. Marine Harley Toney was one of the raiders. "The unit came upon a house. I went in to look around and as I passed by a window, I was shot and wounded in the neck by a sniper in a tree. The bullet sounded as if it hit a metal window sash about the same time as it hit me. The other Marines shot the sniper. The corpsman treated me, told me to lie outside, and said they would get me out under cover of darkness. Sometime later another enemy was shooting at me. I knew that one of us would not survive. I got in a good shot and that ended the encounter." (Courtesy of Harley Toney.)

Toney was evacuated to New Zealand on a hospital ship. He went to a field hospital for surgery and recuperation. When the piece of ammunition was later removed because it was in a muscle and the muscle movement caused soreness; it was a .25-caliber Japanese bullet. Harley H. Toney of the Marine Corps returned to service with an artillery company after he recuperated. The photograph shows him doing duty in the United States. (Courtesy of Harley Toney.)

After capturing a Japanese communications command post, a Marine patrol takes a break on one of the Solomon Islands. This photograph well illustrates the rugged terrain the Marines had to follow. (Courtesy of the United States Marine Corps.)

These Marines are firing a 75-mm pack howitzer on Guadalcanal. The smoke is coming from their own gun in the fighting of November 21, 1942. During the continuing battle, the Marines fought off the desperate Japanese attacks and recaptured Henderson Field. (Courtesy of the United States Marine Corps.)

Adm. A.W. Fitch (in the center) and Gen. Roy S. Geiger (left), who commanded the Marine Air Group on Guadalcanal, take a look around Tulagi Island, which had been occupied by the Japanese in May 1942. The Navy and Marines laid claim to Florida Island, Gavutu, Tanambogo, and Tulagi Island on the same day as the invasion of Guadalcanal. The Japanese did not surrender these areas easily, and troops faced a long series of heavy air, ground, and sea assaults to maintain their treasures. Instead of a single event, the battles became a major campaign for the next four months. By November 1942 the Japanese began to retreat from the islands claimed by American forces. (Courtesy of the United States Marine Corps.)

While the land battles raged on Guadalcanal, the Navy fought a series of five battles with the Japanese fleet. The Battle of Savo Island (August 9, 1942) was the first-ever night fleet engagement, the first-ever defeat in a fleet action, and the worst-ever defeat for the United States Navy, except for Pearl Harbor. The Japanese sank four heavy cruisers and one destroyer. The American losses were 1,270 men killed, 709 wounded; the Japanese losses were negligible. One of the cruisers lost was the *Vincennes*, which was sunk by gunfire from Japanese cruisers on August 9, 1942. The photograph above shows the *Vincennes* at Peal Harbor. (Courtesy of United States Navy.)

On the sinking *Vincennes*, Machinist's Mate Worth Morgan "found a hole in the hull and dived through it. I swam to a life raft and was afloat eight hours before being rescued." Morgan received a Purple Heart as a result of this action. (Courtesy of Worth Morgan.)

The Japanese tried to reinforce their garrison on Guadalcanal with troops ferried on cruisers and destroyers. Adm. Norman Scott's task force ambushed the Japanese force near Cape Esperance on the night of October 11–12, 1942. After a 30-minute battle, the Japanese forces withdrew. This was the first victory in fleet action since 1898. This Japanese ship is a victim of the Battle of Esperance. (Courtesy of the United States Navy.)

November 12–13, 1942, saw the renewal of the surface actions off Guadalcanal (First Naval Battle of Guadalcanal). The Japanese battleships overmatched the American force of cruisers and destroyers. This battle cost the Navy the lives of Rear Adm. Norman Scott of the *Atlanta* and Rear Adm. Dan Callaghan of the *San Francisco*. Both received the Medal of Honor posthumously. (Courtesy of the United States Navy.)

The Second Naval Battle of Guadalcanal occurred on the night of November 14–15, 1942. Unfortunately, the USS *Juneau* sank in this action, and the five Sullivan brothers died. Adm. Willis Lee, the premier American battleship admiral of World War II, defeated the Imperial Japanese *Kirishima.* The USS *South Dakota* pounded the *Kirishima* into a flaming wreck with nine 16-inch hits and about forty 5-inch hits. As a result of these ferocious surface actions, the sound of water between Guadalcanal and Savo Island received the nickname "Iron Bottom Sound." (Courtesy of the United States Navy.)

The Battle for Guadalcanal was also the occasion for two carrier battles: the Battle of the Eastern Solomons (August 23–25, 1942) and the Battle of Santa Cruz Island (October 26, 1942). This picture shows the flight deck of the USS *Wasp* as it prepares to launch its Wildcat fighters during the Battle of Eastern Solomon Islands. (Courtesy of the United States Navy.

During the Battle of Santa Cruz (October 26, 1942), the United States Navy lost its aircraft carrier USS *Hornet* to the torpedo planes and dive-bombers of Japan. (Courtesy of the United States Navy.)

The Battle of Santa Cruz attacks left the *Hornet* dead in the water. Machinist's Mate Fred Owensby Morgan died when the ship received numerous bomb/torpedo hits. Morgan received the Purple Heart posthumously. (Courtesy of Worth Morgan.)

The final offensive on Guadalcanal began on January 15, 1943; this photograph shows Marines engaged in the task of "mopping up" the island. The Japanese lost 6,000 troops; Americans took only 100 prisoners. The Marines lost 1,242, had fewer than 200 captured, and had 2,655 wounded in the 6-month operation. (Courtesy of the United States Marine Corps.)

As the land battle progressed, reinforcements were necessary. Some of the first soldiers drafted and trained received orders for Guadalcanal. One of these men was Vernon Lowery (June 9, 1921–January 28, 1943). Lowery was killed 11 months to the day after his enlistment and just a few days before the end of the Guadalcanal Campaign. (Courtesy of Billy Seay.)

"I remember when James Lowery (a brother to Vernon) came to our house and told my mom (Vernon's sister) that Vernon had been killed. I remember Mom screaming and crying. That was sad. Vernon and Rosewell Wyatt were sweethearts before he went into the U.S. Army. Rosewell never married and still lives in the same house in Henrietta." (Courtesy of Billy Seay.)

Despite the distances and the combat conditions, mail call for the Army and Marines was amazingly regular on the Solomon Islands and Guadalcanal. The postal clerk, unfortunately, often had the unpleasant duty of marking some of the envelopes "Killed in Action" and adding the instruction "Return to Sender." The above envelope was just such an unhappy reminder of the casualties of war. (Photograph courtesy of Billy Seay.)

In early 1943 actors Ray Bolger and Joe E. Brown (representing the USO) came to Guadalcanal. The entertainers put on a two-hour show for the men and even acted as their own stagehands. The men, of course, received them eagerly. (Courtesy of the the United States Marine Corps.)

On February 10, 1943, the Allies—and the United States, in particular—were, after six months, able to announce the conquest of Guadalcanal. This was a severe loss to the Japanese. The campaign had cost the enemy 75,000 men, 800 aircraft, and 166 transports and warships. These Marines were now able to rest 9,000 miles from home on a bench; the sign reads that the bench was just "for you. Try it. It feels better than it looks. Stop and chew the fat." (Courtesy of the United States Marine Corps.)

One line that most enlisted personnel did not mind was that for chow! Everett Blanton sent this photograph home to show his exalted position in line: second. Everett entered service before the bombing of Pearl Harbor. His stations included Illinois and, later, the Aleutian Islands. (Courtesy of Mae Blanton.)

An activity that most enlisted personnel of World War II knew well was marching. Here Everett Blanton and other enlisted men in the 906th Quartermaster Unit participate in a road march. James Everett Blanton is the one on the left rear. (Courtesy of Mae Blanton.)

# *Five*

# Morocco, Algeria, Tunisia (1942–1943)

## Confronting Rommel in the Desert

*On November 8, 1942, United States Army troops, under the command of Maj. Gen. George S. Patton, waded ashore and liberated Morocco in three days.*

President Franklin Delano Roosevelt believed that an invasion of North Africa should be a first step towards an invasion of Europe. On November 8, 1942, the Allies' amphibious attacks (Operation Torch) hit three beaches: the Atlantic coast of Morocco and both Oran and Algiers in Algeria. (Courtesy of the United States Army.)

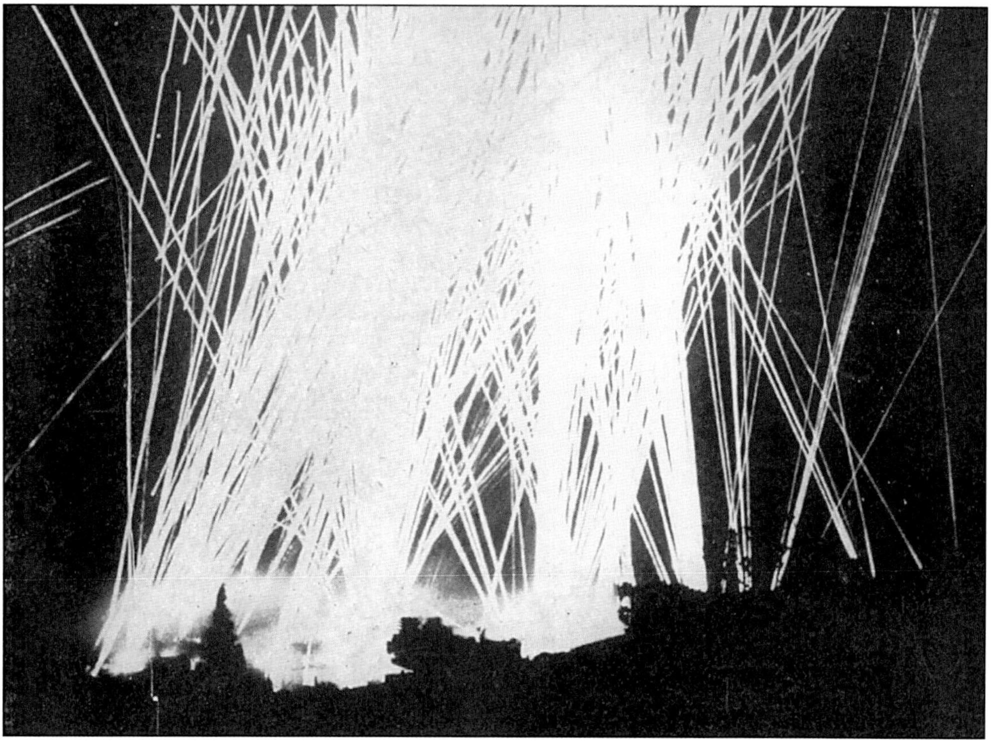

Additionally, 500 transports and 350 ships were on their way to French North Africa, an unknown destination for most of the passengers. Powerful air cover protected the convoy. On November 7–8, 1942, the troops stormed ashore. The landings provided a second front for Americans and prevented the enemy a starting point in the area. This photograph shows an anti-aircraft barrage against the night bombings by the Axis powers. Between November 8 and November 20, the Allies brought down 83 German planes. (Courtesy of the United States Navy.)

The Second Armored Division with Rutherford County native Jack Flack landed at Casablanca, Morocco, on December 24, 1942. The group had made a 12-day voyage from the United States. Flack's unit soon moved to Rabat, Morocco. The Second Armored did not see combat in North Africa. They trained and conducted patrols among the native tribes. (Courtesy of the United States Army.)

To move supplies to the front, the Army used railway operating battalions. Harl Owens was in the 727th Railway Operating Battalion. He served as company cook. His unit supplied hot meals for the troops. Breakfast every day for three years was coffee, powdered eggs, milk, bacon, and oatmeal. Lunch was coffee/tea, a meat, two vegetables, and dessert—usually canned fruit. Supper duplicated the noon meal. Food preparation was on gas-powered ranges. The men, when possible, ate under a large tent. Cleanup of the utensils was in a five-gallon can of hot water. (Courtesy of Harl Owens.)

At first the French resisted the landings of Americans and British troops in French North Africa, but later they offered little resistance. The photograph shows a United States Army Stuart Tank in North Africa. Before long, however, German troops began to pour into Tunisia. On November 15, 1942, French troops joined the Allies. After a long retreat from Egypt, German Field Marshal Erwin Rommel arrived in February of 1943 with British Lt. Gen. B.L. Montgomery close behind. What followed was the battle for the Kasserine Pass where the raw American soldiers received a bloody nose. Recovering quickly under the leadership of Maj. Gen. George S. Patton, American troops pushed Rommel and his Afrika Korps northward. (Courtesy of the United States Army Signal Corps.)

In the advance on Tunisia, the First Infantry Division of the United States Army escorted the Italian prisoners whom they seized on the Tunisian advance to a stockade. (Courtesy of the United States Army Signal Corps.)

In early May 1943, the end of the conflict in North Africa was in sight. Although the surrender was quick in coming, the fighting had been ferocious. Tanks, naval forces, planes from overhead, heavy artillery, and the determination of the troops brought an early victory for the Allies. The accuracy of the aerial bombing was evident when Allied troops entered Tunis after its May 12–13, 1943, surrender. Here a railway depot and other facilities are completely wrecked while the rest of the city was hardly touched. (Courtesy of United States Army Air Forces.)

# Six

# New Guinea, Tarawa, Sicily, the Invasion of Italy (1943–1944)

## Fighting Hard

*New Guinea natives rarely came from the bush into the camp of American servicemen. Here, however, Sgt. George Henson, 43rd Infantry, shares a light moment with the natives. (Courtesy of George Henson.)*

Heat, mud, disease, decay, and little recognition for the American servicemen characterized the New Guinea campaign. Although the conflict continued for months, the news media neglected the United States Army and its sacrifices in the steaming jungles and hostile terrain.

George Henson frequently was first scout on the point of his reconnaissance patrol in New Guinea. He recalls once having heard undecipherable voices in the bush ahead. Calling his sergeant, they listened and decided it was not the Japanese language. Waving their arms, four almost-naked men rose up; Henson and his squad identified them as Indian Prisoners of War from the British garrison at Singapore. The emaciated men, covered with sores, had escaped a Japanese slave-labor camp and were trying to reach American lines and safety. (Courtesy of the United States Army.)

Sergeant Henson remembered another time and place when his unit had been eating mutton three times per day. His friend "Pappy" told George, "If you keep lookout, I will get us some onions from the supply tent." They used these delicacies to supplement their dreary diets. "They were the best onions I have ever had in my life," George remembers. In the photograph above, one can see the supply tent of a New Guinea kitchen with the sides raised; duck boards to walk upon have been placed about the tent so that the thick mud would not suck at one's boots. (Courtesy of George Henson.)

While American Army troops under the command of Gen. Douglas MacArthur continued their clearance of New Guinea, in November 1943 the Second U.S. Marine Division and the Army's 27th Infantry Division invaded Tarawa and Makin in the Gilbert Islands. Units of the United States Navy supplied covering gunfire. (Courtesy of the United States Navy.)

Marines approaching Tarawa Island knew immediately in November 1943 that the conquest would be difficult because the Japanese, strongly entrenched in palm-tree log bunkers, would fight to the death. Out of 4,836 Japanese on the islands, only 146 survived. The United States Army suffered 3,300 casualties and 900 deaths. (Courtesy of the United States Marine Corps.)

Dawn brought Marines to the enemy shore. Marines wade in waist-deep water to reach the beach at Bougainville on November 1, 1943, the opening day of the drive to seize this vital island. (Courtesy of the Marine Corps.)

Harold Hawkins, 21st Marine Regiment, 3rd U.S. Marine Division, was killed weeks into the campaign (December 16, 1943) to liberate Bougainville Island. Hawkins volunteered on September 19, 1942. His family did not find out the details of his demise until after the end of the war. (Courtesy of his brother Lawrence Miller Hawkins.)

On July 9, 1943, the Allies conducted "Operation Husky" (the invasion of Sicily). Taking part was the United States Army's First Infantry Division. Landing with the first wave at Gela was Armond Hutchins. As his unit moved inland, he remembers the rock-hard ground as they tried to dig their foxholes under German fire. They called for Naval gunfire support, which broke up the attack. Armond lost a good friend in action. (Courtesy of the United States Navy.)

The interior of Sicily was barren ground, with olive vineyards and fields enclosed by stonewalls. To move ammunition and food forward, the Army used mules, which were sure-footed enough to traverse the broken terrain. (Courtesy of the United States Army.)

Jack Flack, Company D, 41st Armored Infantry, Second Armored Division, remembers the invasion of Sicily being preceded by a great storm and the seasickness that everyone suffered. His company commander was in charge of a liberated Sicilian town. (Courtesy of Jack Flack.)

German troops blew up as many bridges as they could. United States combat engineers, according to Armond Hutchins, used bulldozers "to make their way through blown bridges." Hutchins recalled that the campaign took 38 days to clear the island. He remembers the beauty of the interior of the cathedral in Messina. He also recalls the cadavers in the catacombs. (Courtesy of the United States Army.)

At the conclusion of the campaign, Jack Flack's Second Armored Division and Armond Hutchins's First Infantry Division were re-deployed to England for the coming invasion of France. Armond Hutchins (first on left) appears here with friends before the French invasion. (Courtesy of Armond Hutchins.)

After the success of the Sicilian operations, Allied forces on September 8, 1943, invaded southern Italy at Salerno. The tenacious German forces created a nightmare for the invaders for nearly a week. The Allied forces slowly advanced on Naples. (Courtesy of the United States Army.)

In a bold move to cut off the German retreat, the Allies landed at Anzio Beach on January 22, 1944. For many days the artillery fire from the notorious Anzio Annie, the 280-mm German Railway Gun that could fire from a range of 38,500 meters, kept the Allies pinned down. Slowly the Allies advanced up the Italian peninsula. Aided by the terrain and the weather, the German defense became even more formidable. (Courtesy of the United States Navy.)

Lt. Gen. Mark W. Clark (third from left and examining the map) led the United States Fifth Army as it broke out from the Anzio Beachhead on May 23, 1944. Clark's army liberated Rome on June 4, 1944. (Courtesy of the United States Army.)

Among the American forces taking part in the liberation of Rome was Tech. Sgt. Harl Owens's 727th Railway Operating Battalion. Owens, Battalion Mess Sergeant, was responsible for procurement of foodstuffs, repair of the mess equipment, and the issue of rations to smaller detachments. He remembers that mess units were usually located beside the railway stations. Owens continued serving in the Army until 1945. (Courtesy of the United States Army.)

Allen Jobe served with the Fifth Army in the Signal Corps. Trained at Fort McClellan, Alabama, Jobe arrived in Naples. While on temporary duty, he was assigned to a barn stacked waist-high with mail. Jobe and his work detail were able to organize the mass of mail and get it on its way to service personnel, eager for messages from home. (Courtesy of Allen Jobe.)

Because of his success in making order of this havoc, Allen Jobe received the assignment as a teletype operator in the Signal Corps. Teletype operators passed coded messages to and from the front-an essential service of command and control. (Courtesy of the United States Army.)

While in Florence, Italy, on April 12, 1945, Jobe was on the Ponte Vecchio over the Arno River; this was the only bridge in Florence spared during World War II. He received the news of President Roosevelt's death on that bridge. He still remembers "there was not a dry eye in the formation." (Courtesy of Charles Morgan, Converse College.)

Alvin Dewit Melton, Fifth Army, 34th Infantry Division, entered service in October 1943 when he was only 17. The orphan "had never been anywhere and felt my world was turned upside down when I was sent all the way to Texas." Melton would be going even further from Rutherford County. He served his county and nation in England, France, and Italy. (Courtesy of Alvin Dewit Melton.)

No matter where American service personnel were stationed, mail from home was important. Here James Everett Blanton smiles as he reads a message from home. (Courtesy of Mae Blanton.)

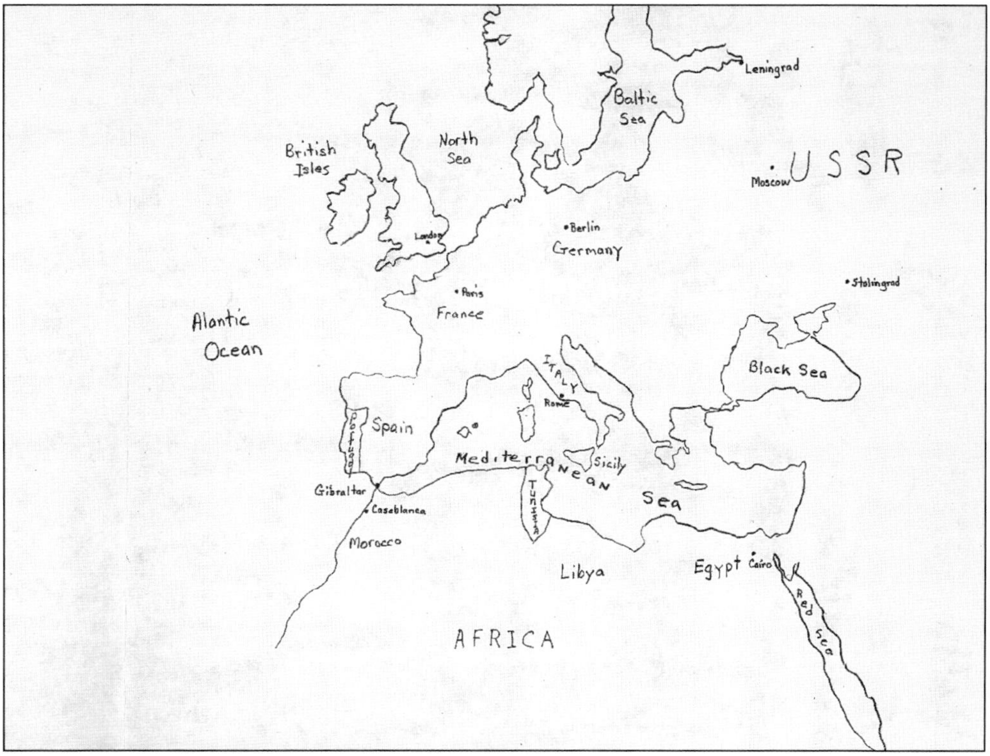


This sketch-map shows areas of operation in the Mediterranean Theater. (Courtesy of James M. Walker.)

Logan Martin, 1530th G/S Engineer Company, served in North Africa and Italy. Martin was awarded three battle stars for his service in Italy. General Service Engineers were responsible for the construction of air fields, roads, campsites, etc. Martin remembers he was close enough to the front lines that he could see the smoke and hear the fire of the artillery. (Courtesy of Logan Martin.)

*Seven*

# Central Pacific Islands, Burma, D-Day, Leyte Island, Battle of Bulge (1944–1945)

## Liberating the Oppressed

*The year 1944 saw the United States Army and the United States Navy advancing across the vast stretch of the Pacific and driving the Japanese toward their home islands. In that same year Gen. Douglas MacArthur kept his promise and returned to the Philippines. In the European Theater, years of training and preparation achieved fruition with the massive invasion of Normandy.*

Here 53 inductees from Rutherford County line the steps of the courthouse in Rutherfordton on November 3, 1942. These young men would enter all branches of service and locate in areas from the Atlantic to the Pacific. (Courtesy of Armond Hutchins.)

The massive numbers of aircraft carriers used to pound the determined Japanese characterized the Central Pacific Campaign. Current Rutherford County resident Gilbert Mays served as pilot of a United States Navy TBM torpedo bomber on board the carrier *Yorktown*. (Courtesy of Gilbert Mays.)

Gilbert Mays was a part of Torpedo Squadron One on the *Yorktown*. This was the whimsical insignia of Torpedo One. (Courtesy of Gilbert Mays.)

This photograph shows Lt. Gilbert Mays preparing for takeoff in his TBM Torpedo Bomber. (Courtesy of Gilbert Mays.)

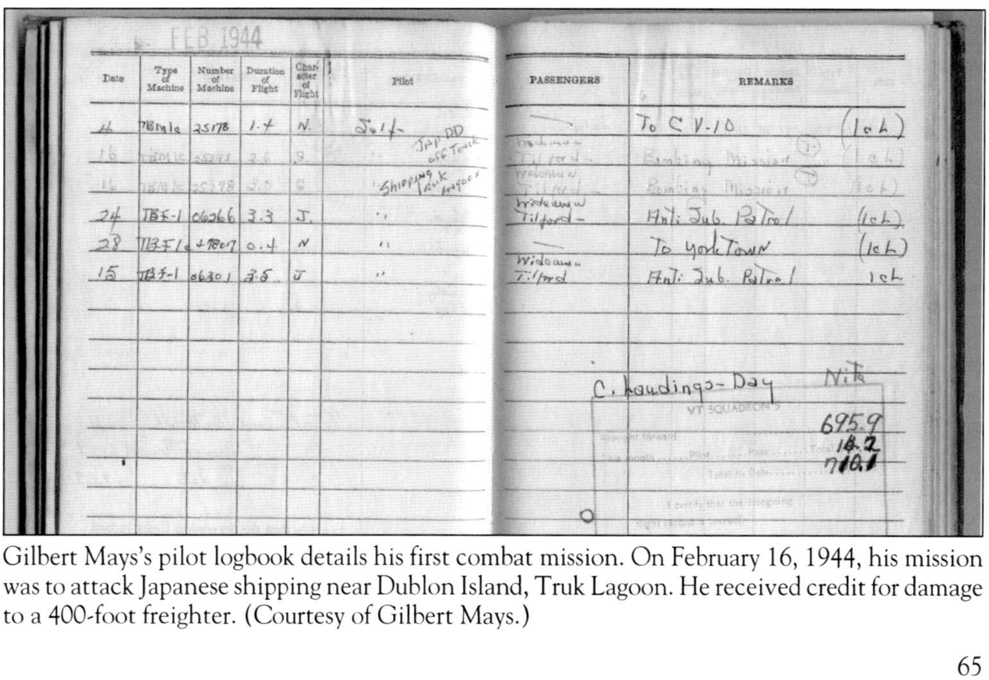

FEB 1944

| Date | Type of Machine | Number of Machine | Duration of Flight | Character of Flight | Pilot | Passengers | Remarks |
|---|---|---|---|---|---|---|---|
| 4 | TBM1c | 25178 | 1.4 | N. | Self | | To CV-10 (1cL) |
| 16 | TBM1c | 25271 | 2.6 | | " JAP DD off Truk | Widemann Tilford | Bombing Mission (1cL) |
| 16 | TBM1c | 25178 | 3.0 | | " Shipping Truk Lagoon | Widemann Tilford | Bombing Mission (1cL) |
| 24 | TBF-1 | 06266 | 3.3 | J. | " | Widemann Tilford | Anti Sub. Patrol (1cL) |
| 28 | TBF1c | 47807 | 0.4 | N | " | | To YorkTown (1cL) |
| 15 | TBF-1 | 06301 | 3.5 | J | " | Widemann Tilford | Anti Sub. Patrol 1cL |

C. Landings - Day Nite

VT SQUADRON

695.9
14.2
710.1

Gilbert Mays's pilot logbook details his first combat mission. On February 16, 1944, his mission was to attack Japanese shipping near Dublon Island, Truk Lagoon. He received credit for damage to a 400-foot freighter. (Courtesy of Gilbert Mays.)

The Japanese Imperial Fleet made use of the fine natural harbor of Truk Lagoon, the principal Japanese base in the Central Pacific. Freighters used Dublon Island as an anchorage point before supplying Japanese outposts. This photo shows some of the many islands that made up the lagoon. (Courtesy of Gilbert Mays.)

In an effort to keep their Chinese allies in the war, Lt. Gen. Joseph W. Stilwell (left) in Burma used 5307th Composite Unit (Provisional), under the command of Brig. Gen. Frank Merrill (right), to attack Japanese forces at Walawbum, Burma. The 5307th Composite Unit (Merrill's Marauders) was an all-volunteer unit and included Rutherford County native Paul Toney. The Marauders endured poor diet, tainted water, blood-sucking leeches, and the ever-present Japanese. (Courtesy of the United States Signal Corps.)

Paul Toney volunteered in late 1943 from the 25th Infantry Division and was sent from New Georgia Island, via Australia, to Bombay, India. He underwent jungle training with the 5307th Composite Unit in Assam Province. His most vivid memory was near Nhpum Gap where his unit (Third Battalion) relieved the Second Battalion, which the Japanese had besieged for 14 days. Toney recalls the horror of seeing body parts from his comrades hanging from trees after the Japanese mortar and artillery attacks. He shared this memory with the authors on April 9, 2003, the 59th anniversary of the occasion. (Courtesy of Paul Toney.)

Some of the Marauders manage to barbecue deer meat in Burma. (Courtesy of the United States Army.)

An officer of the 5307th Composite Unit (Merrill's Marauders) receives his issue of "K" rations near Naubum, Burma, on April 29, 1941. His unit is preparing for a long, hard march. (Courtesy of the United States Army.)

Charlie L. Queen was one of the first men to volunteer from Rutherford County for duty in World War II. He was in the 254th Ordnance Battalion. Queen was trained as a supply sergeant who, with countless others, supplied troops with field equipment. Queen is shown here with (left to right) Eddie Gominc and Willard Elliott; Queen is the third from left. The scene is Lake Erie, Ohio. (Courtesy of Charlie L. Queen.)

Queen carried a Bible that Mr. Dee Harrill had gotten from a World War I veteran. Mr. Harrill told Queen to take it to England and bring it back home with him. (Courtesy of Charlie L. Queen.)

After a buildup of two-and-a-half years, Allied forces were ready to attempt the invasion of Hitler's Europe. The United States Army had deployed thousands of troops to South England for the coming invasion of Normandy, France. At various bases throughout Southern England, the Allied high commanders brought the troops' enthusiasm to a fever pitch. The C-47 Pathfinder Crews at Aldermaston Air Base near Reading, England, listen intently to Air Chief Marshal Sir Trafford Leigh-Mallory. Leeman Ray Pegram has labeled himself in the back row. (Courtesy of Leeman Ray Pegram.)

On the night of June 5–6, 1944, Paratroopers of the 82nd and 101st Airborne Divisions dropped from C-47s behind the invasion beaches. Staff Sgt. Ray Pegram, radio operator, and the crew of the C-47 "Butch" appear here prior to flight. Pegram is the fifth from the left. (Courtesy of Leeman Ray Pegram.)

The Allied forces invaded five separate beaches in France. At 6:00 a.m. on June 6, on the beach codenamed "Omaha," the 18th regiment of the First Infantry Division disembarked from their landing craft into neck-deep water. The seasick, disoriented men struggled up "the gravel shingle" toward shore. They dodged among German obstacles, tried to avoid land mines, and all the while were aware of the murderous machinegun cross fire and artillery explosions. Wounded men were begging for help as they lay wounded; many drowned with their 80-pound packs still on their backs. (Courtesy of Armond Hutchins and the United States Army.)

Company A, First Battalion, 18th Infantry Regiment, 1st Infantry Division, was finally able to advance from the beach after neutralizing German pillboxes with machine guns and anti-tank guns. Allied weapons included flamethrowers, satchel charges, and Bangalore torpedoes. Staff Sgt. Armond Hutchins miraculously survived D-Day unwounded. (Courtesy of Armond Hutchins.)

Casualties were high on Omaha Beach. Private First Class Walter R. Owens of the Second Infantry Division suffered a severe head wound as his landing craft approached shore. He was evacuated to England, but doctors were unable to remove the metal fragments. He carried them with him the rest of his life. (Photograph courtesy of his daughter Patricia Owens Anders; Mrs. Edith Owens helped with gathering the information.)

To transport the enormous quantities of heavy equipment across the Channel, Allied forces used all types of landing craft. This photograph shows the LST 55 carrying a full load of trucks and departing Plymouth, England. (Courtesy of William Keller.)

After unloading the cargo, the LSTs would be reconfigured to evacuate the wounded to hospitals in England. Seaman First Class William Keller served as a crewman on LST 55, which carried many wounded. Keller still recalls "the stoic behavior in the face of mortal wounds as the young men were evacuated." (Courtesy of William Keller.)

Subsequent to securing the beachhead, a steady stream of reinforcements arrived from England. On D+4, the Second Armored Division was deployed to France. Among these was Staff Sgt. Jack Flack's Company D, 41st Infantry. Flack assisted his company commander by keeping field maps to record enemy positions. (Courtesy of Jack Flack.)

On D+13, the 83rd Infantry Division arrived. Staff Sgt. Troy H. Mayse began the first of 276 days and nights in a foxhole. Sergeant Mayse commanded a 60-mm mortar unit of 18 men. While serving with the 331st Infantry Regiment, Mayse participated in five campaigns: Normandy, Northern France, Ardennes, the Rhineland, and Central Europe. Mayse received the Combat Infantryman's Badge (CIB), the Bronze Star, and the Purple Heart. As his Colonel pinned the CIB on Mayse, the Colonel said, "Sergeant, you ought to have a home in heaven. You have had hell here on earth." (Courtesy of Troy Mayse.)

Another serving in Normandy during the hedgerow campaign was Falls W. Price, who served as medic for his unit. A vivid memory is that of "Bed Check Charlie," a German bomber that harassed them each night. (Courtesy of Falls W. Price.)

An often unsung unit was the Combat Engineer. One of these soldiers was Pfc. James Monroe Morrow, Sr. His unit-Company D, 373rd Combat Engineers-was responsible for building pontoon bridges, constructing airstrips, and clearing mines. Near Le Harve, France, this unit deactivated over 3,000 mines in the city and its docks. (Courtesy of James Monroe Morrow Sr. and Beverly Gordon.)

Hedgerows six to eight feet tall and usually impenetrable to the individual soldier marked the Normandy landscape. These man-made barriers had been cultivated for generations to divide the pasture land. The Germans, however, used them as a highly effective barrier to Allied troop movement. Concealed by the hedgerows, the Germans would place machine guns at each end of the barriers to delay the Allied breakout and inflict numerous casualties. This photograph shows members of the HQ Company D, 41st Armored Infantry among the hedgerows. Staff Sgt. Jack Flack is the fourth from left in the back row. (Courtesy of Jack Flack.)

On July 25, 1944, the Allied forces launched Operation COBRA. This operation was undertaken to unleash American Army forces west of the city of St. Lo, France. The attack was preceded by massive bombing strikes, which demolished the city and reduced parts of it to a virtual moonscape. (Courtesy of Mike Davis.)

After blasting apart the German front line during Operation COBRA, American Army troops poured through the gap. One of these units was the 30th Infantry Division in which Sgt. Roy Price served. Price was wounded in the attack. After treatment, he returned to service with the 980th Ordnance Company. (Courtesy of Beverly Manous Price.)

The United States Army has always been lavish in its support personnel. Exemplifying this "support" were units as diverse as photo-interpretation units, field-artillery units with howitzers and guns as large as 8 inches, and railway operating battalions. With the success of Operation COBRA, Lt. Gen. George S. Patton's Third Army was activated. Following in the Army's wake was Sgt. Mike Davis of the 19th Photo Tech. Davis recalls after the St. Lo attacks, "The U.S. personnel killed in action were buried in mattress covers." (Courtesy of Mike Davis.)

August of 1944 saw Lieutenant General Patton's Third Army unleashed. His units besieged the Occupied French port of Brest. Serving with the 740th Field Artillery was Pfc. John Brooks. (Courtesy of John Brooks.)

Brooks's unit was equipped with massive 8-inch howitzers, which took a 27-pound powder charge to fire. These powerful weapons helped to reduce the German defenses. Here Brooks (with pistol) poses with an M2 .50 machine gun. (Courtesy of John Brooks.)

The Second Armored Division pressed forward from St. Lo to the vicinity of Mortain. While Patton's Third Army cleared the Brittany Peninsula, separate American forces encircled over 100,000 German troops in the Falaise-Mortain's pocket. Here Jack Flack stands before a camouflaged jeep just outside St. Lo. (Courtesy of Jack Flack.)

Sgt. Charles Vess, 501st Parachute Regiment, 101st Airborne Division, unwinds in London at Trafalgar Square. His unit was withdrawn from Normandy to rest, refit, and recuperate after the arduous combat. (Courtesy of Charles Vess.)

Because of the Germans' defensive collapse, the roads to Paris and the upper Seine were open. America and the Free French Forces raced to liberate the "City of Light." Here T-4 Al Lancaster, Battery B, 182nd Field Artillery Battalion, stands on the banks of the Seine River in August 1944. (Courtesy of Al Lancaster.)

Ecstatic French girls swarm the cobblestone streets of Paris in August of 1944. Here they welcome the 2nd Battalion, 110th Regiment, 28th Division troops who helped to liberate the French capital. (Courtesy of Mike Davis.)

Although few United States Army troops saw Paris liberated, Falls Price was able to do so. The majority of the troops, however, remained on the line to push German troops closer to the Fatherland. Pfc. Timer Tessneer of Company B, 546th Field Artillery, attached to the Third Army, was one of those remaining on the line. (Courtesy of Timer Tessneer.)

To move vast amounts of supplies from the Normandy Beachhead, the United States Army organized several railway operating battalions. One of these was the 720th Railway Operating Battalion, which went ashore on D+14. J.T. Doty served with this unit. A favorite story of J.T. Doty is how he was standing in an apple orchard in Cherbourg, France, when he heard his nickname being shouted from the window of a moving train. When the engineer called out, "Jeter-r-r-r-r-r-r," the sound echoed as the train moved into the distance. Later that same day, the engineer came back to that area to find his friend from Ellenboro. The engineer was Ivey Ray Mauney. The two had a joyous reunion. (Courtesy of J.T. Doty.)

T-5 Ivey Ray Mauney's 718th Railway Operating Battalion had gone ashore at Utah Beach on D+70 (August 15, 1944) and was soon operating trains on the liberated French Railway System. The unit transported fuel, rations, and heavy equipment. Mauney's main duty was that of a locomotive engineer. (Courtesy of Ivey Ray Mauney.)

In September and October, the Allies advanced to the German borders in the east and to Belgium and Luxembourg in the north. With the rapidity of the American advance, the supplies diminished quickly. The advance ground to a halt; this pause gave the Germans a chance to reorganize, refit, and reinforce their shattered forces. Falls Price was one of the troops who moved into Belgium when gasoline arrived. Here he stands in Belgium with a friend; in the background is the 2.5-ton truck. This deuce-and-a-half was truly a ubiquitous vehicle. (Courtesy of Falls W. Price.)

In the summer of 1944 the United States Pacific fleet continued its drive across the island chains of the Central Pacific. Concurrently, the forces of Gen. Douglas MacArthur completed its advance on New Guinea. The stage was now set for the liberation of the Philippines and MacArthur's return. This photograph shows one of the numerous Japanese airbases that dotted the islands of the Pacific. Navy aviators damaged severely the Japanese air forces. (Courtesy of Gilbert Mays.)

The Mariana Islands were stepping stones to the Philippine Islands. In the middle of June 1944, the United States Navy invaded the island called Saipan. This invasion called for a response from the Imperial Japanese Fleet. The result of the battle that ensued was 426 Japanese planes destroyed and three carriers sunk. Taking part in this great three-day battle (the Battle of the Philippine Sea) was the USS *Biloxi*. One of its crew was Seaman First Class Dwight ("Buck") Green. (Courtesy of Dwight Green.)

After securing Saipan and capturing neighboring Tinian Island, the United States forces garrisoned the islands. One of the facilities on Saipan was 176th Station Hospital where T-4 Zeno Toney was a medical clerk. Toney remembers an occasion when a small group of Japanese soldiers walked out of the hills and surrendered in front of the hospital. (Courtesy of Zeno Toney.)

On October 20, 1944, American forces invaded Leyte Island in the south Philippines. MacArthur had returned! The Sixth Army of the United States came ashore with more than 130,000 men. One of these was Pfc. James S. Seay, Battery C, 117th Field Artillery Battalion. Private Seay's duty was that of a cannoneer of an 8-inch artillery piece, which he fired. (Courtesy of Billy Seay.)

Another soldier taking part in the invasion of Leyte was Pfc. Lawrence Miller Hawkins of the 96th Infantry Division. Here Hawkins appears with fellow soldiers (from left to right, L.D. Stiden, Bill DeRossett, and Lawrence Hawkins) at San Luis Obispo, California, for pre-invasion training. (Courtesy of Lawrence Miller Hawkins.)

During his interview, James Price recalled "as if it were yesterday" how he and fellow soldier Bob Ross were on patrol on what would later be called "Purple Heart Hill." Price recollects how Ross picked up an d carried back to American lines a light Japanese machine gun (nicknamed the "woodpecker") that he and Price had taken at the ridge. (Courtesy of James Price and the United States Army.)

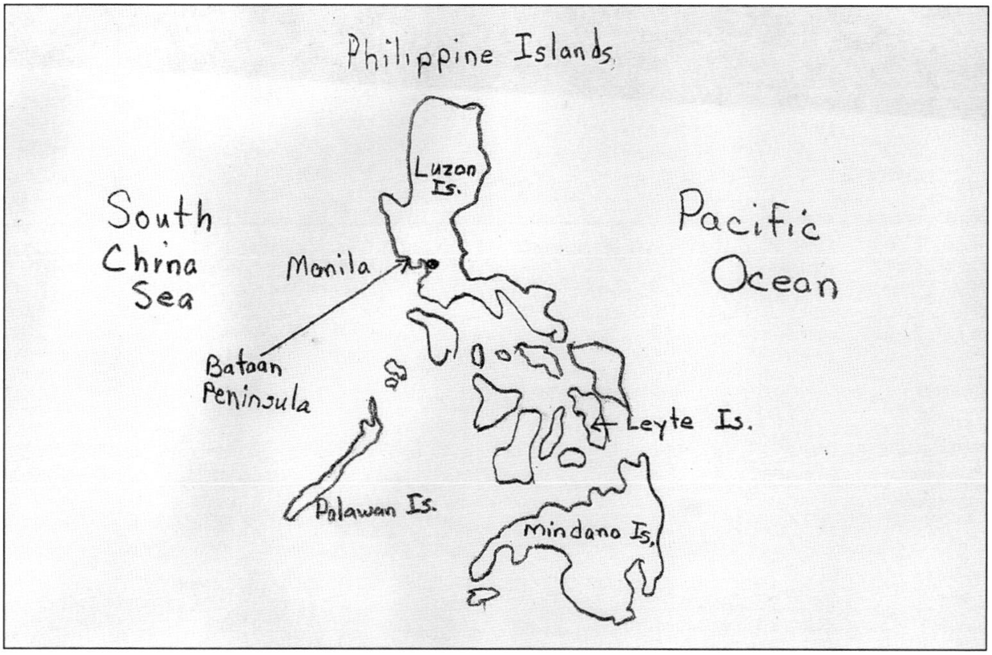


MacArthur's return would not be complete until his soldiers had liberated Luzon, its Bataan Peninsula, and the adjacent Corregidor Island. On January 9, 1945, the Sixth Army landed nearly 100,000 troops at Luzon. The Japanese displayed their usual ferocious defense. (Courtesy of James M. Walker.)

Fellow Rutherford County native Staff Sgt. James Price, Company "C," 152nd Infantry, 38th Infantry Division, describes himself as being "a mean soldier." He recalls that Leyte Island was "the muddiest place I have ever been." Price received the Combat Infantryman's Badge and two Bronze Stars. Sergeant Price's good friend Angel Pla took the photograph. (Courtesy of James Price.)

James Price's best friend from Rutherford County was Pfc. Walter Powell. Powell "shared duty with Price in Company C and during the action on Luzon Island." Company C, 152nd Infantry Regiment, 38th Division, was highly regarded for its accomplishments in the Luzon action. Powell was later wounded by shrapnel at a place nicknamed "Woodpecker Ridge;" the name came from the Japanese machine guns there. Powell (left) is pictured here. James Price is on the right. (Courtesy of Ronnie Powell.)

Here Walter Powell (left) is pictured (before his injury) digging a slit trench on the island. Fellow Rutherford County soldiers Claude Sigmon and Rush Cobb died during "mopping up" operations on Luzon on May 2, 1945, and May 4, 1945, respectively. (Courtesy of James Price and the United States Army.)

Pfc. George Henson receives the Bronze Star from Maj. Gen. Leonard F. Wing, the commanding officer of the 43rd Infantry Division. Henson received his medal for volunteering to search for a fellow soldier who had been wounded in an ambush. Henson found the man who had bled to death and carried the body back to American lines; Henson later found out the soldier was a fellow Tar Heel. (Courtesy of George Henson.)

The final stain of MacArthur's humiliation was Corregidor. To remove the blot, paratroopers of the 503rd Regimental Combat Team air-dropped on the island on February 16, 1945. Jumping from a low altitude, Staff Sgt. Roy McKinney landed in a bomb crater and injured his jaw and chest. The 503rd suffered 170 casualties during the operation of battling 6,000 Japanese troops. This was Sergeant McKinney's third parachute assault of the Pacific War. His other drops were at Lae, New Guinea, and Noemfoor, New Guinea. (Courtesy of Roy McKinney.)

Sgt. Roy McKinney was one of seven brothers to serve in the United States military during the War. Lee McKinney served with the Navy Seabees; John C. McKinney served the Army in Burma; Howard McKinney served with the Army in the Philippines; and Fay McKinney served the Army (no location given). Pictured above are the two brothers KIA. Pvt. Earl McKinney (left) was in the Army and killed in action near Aachen, Germany, on September 22, 1944. Pfc. Broadus M. McKinney (right) was killed on December 11, 1944, in Burma. Up to this time there had been only one incident when a Rutherford County family lost two sons in service in World War II; the other two brothers killed had been Pfc. Toy Ruppe (September 13, 1944) and Pfc. Lynn Ruppe (September 23, 1943), both of Cliffside. Later, another family would know the hurt when Gilkey Addie Hall Jr. (June 7, 1944) and Daniel Kerp Hall (January 25, 1945) were killed. (Courtesy of Roy McKinney.)

As soon as the Philippine areas were secure, the Navy established various patrol bases there. One location was on Porto Princessa on the Palawan Island. From there, William J. Price of the Navy flew patrols in a PB4Y2 (B-24) over the South China Sea; his search was for Japanese submarines and targets of opportunity. At the end of the war, Price's plane was tasked to fly to Korea to return eight Allied Prisoners of War held by the Japanese. (Courtesy of William J. Price.)

By the fall of 1944, the American armies, under the supreme command of Gen. Dwight D. Eisenhower, stood poised to continue the advance into Belgium and Germany. Twelfth Army Group, under the command of Gen. Omar Bradley, divided into the First and Third Army. The First Amy under the command of Lt. Gen. Courtney Hodges was to attack into Belgium and Luxembourg. Gen. George S. Patton's Third Army continued to strive in the region of Nancy and Metz, France. T-5 Willard G. Bradley of Rutherford County is pictured here chauffeuring Gen. Omar Bradley as he inspects troops of the 28th Infantry Division. (Courtesy of Chivous Omar Bradley.)

The first German city that the American troops attacked was Aachen, Germany, in September 1944. South of the city was an evergreen wood known as the Huertgen Forest. Hutchins told of how it seemed the "Germans were behind every tree and every log." The First Infantry Division, 18th Infantry Regiment, was one of the units that attempted to clear the forest. Staff Sgt. Armond Hutchins, Company A, led a reinforced squad of 16 men to attack a German-occupied fire watchtower. Hutchins recalls that although the Germans were "looking right down our throats," he and his men knocked out the tower. At the end of this ordeal, more than 20 Germans lay dead. Out of his 16 men, only 3 were unwounded. This photograph of Hutchins resting in Belgium indicates the terrible strain of combat. (Courtesy of Armond Hutchins.)

Taking the place of the First Infantry (tired from weeks of combat) was the 28th Infantry Division with an attachment of the 8th Cavalry Reconnaissance Troop. On November 15, 1944, the 8th Cavalry moved up to relieve the 28th Infantry. "The conditions were terrible with snow and mud mixed all together on the ground. As they dug in, they discovered the Germans were defending elaborate bomb fortifications and had posted snipers high in the trees." In the hard fighting ahead, Bradley and his fellow soldiers met the fiercest resistance they had seen. The Germans fired their artillery and mortars so they would explode in the treetops and rain shrapnel and tree limbs on the troops below. The American soldiers literally had to hug the tree trunks for protection; the 28th Infantry Division received the nickname "Bucket of Blood" after their horrendous casualties. (Courtesy of Chivous Omar Bradley.)

As November 1944 closed, Allied troops were recovering from the Battle of Huertgen Forest and the campaign in Lorraine, France. Few of the high command thought the Germans were capable of launching a counter-offensive in the west. On December 16, 1944, Hitler launched a major attack through the Ardennes Forest to capture Antwerp, Belgium. In the early day of the battle the American lines were overrun. (Courtesy of Falls W. Price.)

To stem the German advance, General Eisenhower rushed reinforcements into Belgium. One of these units was the 740th Field Artillery. Pfc. John Brooks recalled, "It was so cold you could pull the ice right off your face." He said that in the town of St. Vith, "not a house seemed to be standing." Brooks also related that at the end of the battle, "bodies were stacked like cordwood." (Courtesy of John Brooks.)

To illustrate the vast troop movement, on December 23, 1944, Falls Price was seated in a café in Liege, Belgium. When he glanced up, he saw a soldier who looked like a larger version of the 16-year-old brother he left behind three years ago. It was indeed his brother Arthur Fred Price of Company B, 172nd Combat Engineer Battalion. The two had a wonderful reunion and had their photographs made together. Five days later, Arthur Price was killed. (Courtesy of Carolyn Barbee, Falls Price, and Nell Price Burns [now deceased].)

German forces besieged the American troops in the town of Bastogne. On Christmas Day 1944, good weather returned and allowed airdrops of food, ammunition, and medical supplies. This photograph shows a Troop Carrier Command C-47 of the 71st Squadron/434 Group/9th Air Force dropping supplies to airborne forces at Bastogne. (Courtesy of Ray Pegram.)

Northern attacks led by British Field Marshal Sir B.L. Montgomery and southern attacks led by Lt. Gen. George S. Patton stopped the German drive. Allied forces slowly drove the Germans back and restored the Allied front. This was not done without casualties. Corp. Arthur F. Price of Company B, 172nd Engineer Combat Battalion was killed on December 28, 1944, at a bridge in Germany when his rifle snagged a land mine and detonated. (Courtesy of Carolyn Barbee, Falls Price, and Nell Price Burns [now deceased].)

The winter of 1944–1945 was one of the worst on record. Jack Flack remembers having to dig foxholes in the snow in Belgium. Arthur Price wrote home of the metal of his rifle adhering to his skin in the cold. Armond Hutchins recalled leading a patrol while dressed in white camouflage smocks; the undetected Americans came so close to the German sentries that it seemed that they could have reached out and touched them. (Courtesy of the United States Army.)

Reinforcements and supplies were rushed to the Infantry as they fought at the front. Moving these supplies were the Railway Operating Battalions. The troops of the Railway Operating Battalions worked long hours under hazardous conditions. Here Engineer Berger and J.T. Doty (standing) depart from Herbasthal. (Courtesy of J.T. Doty.)

Even as the Battle of the Bulge raged, operations continued in other areas. One of these was the reduction of the Colmar pocket south of Strasbourg, France. Pvt. John B. Sane, Company B, 15th Infantry Regiment, 3rd Infantry Division was one of the men helping to reduce the pocket. Sane's unit wore an armband on one of the invasions. Sane had served with his unit in Tunisia, Sicily, Italy, through southern France, and finally in the Rhineland. Sane served in the same unit as war-hero Audie Murphy. (Courtesy of Clara Sane.)

The year 1944 drew to an end. Much hard fighting was over. Countless good men had been wounded and many had died. However, there were light moments of humor and moments of relaxation. This humorous scene shows Ray Pegram and the unit mascot being "captured" by George Egany from New York. (Courtesy of Ray Pegram.)

# *Eight*

# Germany, Iwo Jima, Okinawa (1945)

## Prevailing in Europe and Battling in the Pacific

*In the Pacific, the American forces readied themselves to attack Iwo Jima and Okinawa, to open the way to the home islands of Japan. The year of 1945 began with the defeat of the last German counteroffensive in the west. In the east the Soviet Union's Red Army stood on the Oder River and poised to attack Berlin.*

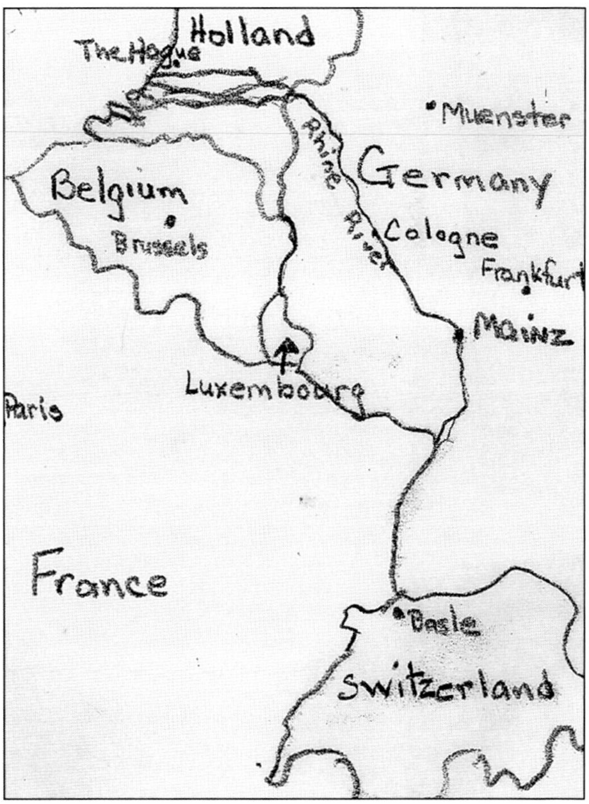


This sketch-map, courtesy of James M. Walker, shows areas of operations on the western front.

In the west, Allied forces pressed the Germans back to the Rhine River. During one of these skirmishes, Sgt. Willard Bradley with another non-com was sent out to scout for casualties. A German fighter strafed Bradley's jeep. Bradley was wounded in the chest by a bullet that entered his body below his heart, penetrated his abdomen, damaged his liver and spleen, and exited the front of his body at his right hip. The wound was so serious that he was evacuated to England. Later Gen. Omar Bradley visited the wounded in the hospital; he showed so much compassion that Willard decided if he had a son, he would name him Omar. Willard's brother-in-law O.L. Lancaster (pictured here on the left) served in the Pacific Theater against the Japanese. (Courtesy of Chivous Omar Bradley.)

Even though Arthur F. Price had written home that "there was one more river to cross and he would be home," he—and others—did not cross that river. Finally, on March 7, 1945, a patrol of the 9th Armored Division seized the Ludendorff Railway Bridge over the Rhine River near Bonn. Attached to the 9th Armored Division were the units of the 656th Tank Destroyer Battalion (SP). Pfc. Thomas Earl Baldwin served in a tank destroyer. The capture of the bridge enabled the American forces to get 8,000 men across the river. This photograph shows Baldwin (right) and a friend beside their vehicle during training in the United States. (Courtesy of Thomas Earl Baldwin.)

With the last natural barrier breached, other units quickly built pontoon bridges across the Rhine. John Brooks's 740th Field Artillery Battalion crossed the above bridge in the advance. (Courtesy of John Brooks.)

In the drive forward, the field artillery units supported the American forces. The Germans greatly feared these powerful weapons and the American's ability to call in massive numbers of guns in a technique known as "Time on Target." Here Al Lancaster (first on left) and his comrades fall out of their tent for duty with their 155-mm howitzer. (Courtesy of Al Lancaster.)

When American forces found worthwhile targets, the artillery would bombard them with a veritable blizzard of shells-all arriving simultaneously. This technique of firing was "Time on Target." This training photograph shows Battery B of the 546th Field Artillery. Timer Tessneer is the first man on the left in the front row. His job on the 155-mm "Long Tom" howitzer was to set the quadrant (raise the barrel up and down). In actual combat Timer remembers one of the men who regularly yelled after each firing, "Now Hitler! Count your men!" (Courtesy of Timer Tessneer.)

Sgt. Mike Davis's 19th Photo Tech Unit followed in the wake of Lieutenant General Patton's Third Army and was briefly quartered in Trier, Germany. While not on duty, Davis went "rabbit hunting" with his M-1 carbine. The "rabbits" were actually hares. Davis, being a crack shot, knocked one head over heels. This photograph shows Davis (standing, right) dressing their kill. The soldiers shared the dressed animals with the hungry civilian children in the area. (Courtesy of Mike Davis.)

The railway operating battalions followed close on the heels of the advancing troops. In an unending quest for more motive power, United States railway troops were sent out to salvage abandoned German locomotives. In early April 1945, T-5 Ivey Ray Mauney (right) was sent out with a squad in a 6-by-6 vehicle. Mauney and his men found a fine 4–8–4 German locomotive. They re-watered the engine by pumping water from an adjacent river. After removing explosive charges from the firebox, Mauney and his men stripped a porch off a nearby German home to fire the locomotive. When the first load of wood was insufficient, Ray used the 6-by-6 to rip a large wooden garage door off its hinges to complete his mission. (Courtesy of Ivey Ray Mauney.)

On the eastern front, the rapid Red Army advance caused large numbers of refugees to head west. Near the city of Frankfort Am Main, Mike Davis observed old men, children, and women with everything they possessed piled into carts as they tried to escape the Russian advance. With tears in his eyes, Mike Davis told the authors, "Pitiful! Pitiful!" (Courtesy of Mike Davis.)

World War II unleashed horrors the world had never seen: death camps where the Nazi regime practiced genocide upon Jews and Hitler's enemies. This Holocaust appalled the troops seeking to liberate the emaciated prisoners. This photograph shows the remains of cremated victims at Buchenwald. The remaining prisoners were liberated on April 11, 1945. (Courtesy of Mike Davis.)

On April 12, 1945, President Franklin Delano Roosevelt died in Warm Springs, Georgia. Vice-President Harry S. Truman then took office. President Truman vowed to continue President Roosevelt's policies of unconditional surrender. With British and American forces closing in from the west and the Red Army assaulting Berlin, Hitler took to his bunker for the final three weeks of his life and of the 1,000-year-old Reich. During the last month of the war, Armond Hutchins (left) of the 1st Infantry Division advanced into Czechoslovakia; he is pictured here in Czechoslovakia. (Courtesy of Armond Hutchins.)

On May 8, 1945, the formal documents of surrender were signed by representatives of the Allied powers and the defeated Germans. The surrender set off wild celebrations that reached echoed around the world. As far away as the Central Pacific island of Tinian, Frank Rossi (seated at right) celebrates in the mess hall. Staff Sergeant Rossi was an Armorer (United States Army Air Forces) and was stationed on Tinian Island. Later known as Frank Wayne in show business, Rossi worked with Mark Goodson and Bill Todman to create and later to produce *Password*. He also helped to create and produce *The Price is Right*. His son Mark Wayne supplied the photographs from his collection in memory of his father.

The conquest of Iwo Jima by United States Marines is the best-known battle of World War II. On the night before the scheduled invasion (February 19, 1945), the USS *Gamble* was offshore. One of those aboard was SM1/C Grover C. Haynes, pictured on the right. The crew would have had a ringside seat to the action on shore had two bombs not struck the *Gamble* at 11 p.m. on February 18, 1945, and "peeled back the deck." Grover Haynes was asleep in his bunk, about 40 feet forward of the boiler room when the bomb hit. (Courtesy of Grover Haynes.)

"Only one bulkhead separated the boiler room from the main ammo compartment as well as our sleeping compartment. Had the bombs hit one foot forward of where they did, I wouldn't be writing this e-mail. The remainder of the night was spent tending to the seven dead and many wounded, getting them off to another ship for treatment, and throwing anything heavy overboard to lighten ship as the 20-foot missing section of our keel put the ship in danger of sinking." (Quote and photograph courtesy of Grover C. Haynes.)

After the horrendous night, Grover Haynes (third from left) and some of the crew posed briefly beside some of the damage on the *Gamble*. (Courtesy of Grover Haynes.)

Blockhouses, pillboxes, "spider holes," and hidden artillery positions studded the five-mile-long island of Iwo Jima. The Japanese occupants realized that they had no hope of victory; their mission was simply to inflict as many casualties as possible before their inevitable demise on the "steak-shaped" island of volcanic ash and black sand. On the morning of February 19, 1945, the 5th Amphibious Corps (the 4th U.S. Marine Division, the 5th U.S. Marine Division, and the 3rd U.S. Marine Division in reserve) landed on the island after a preliminary naval "softening" and 72 days of continuous air bombardment. (Courtesy of the United States Marine Corps.)

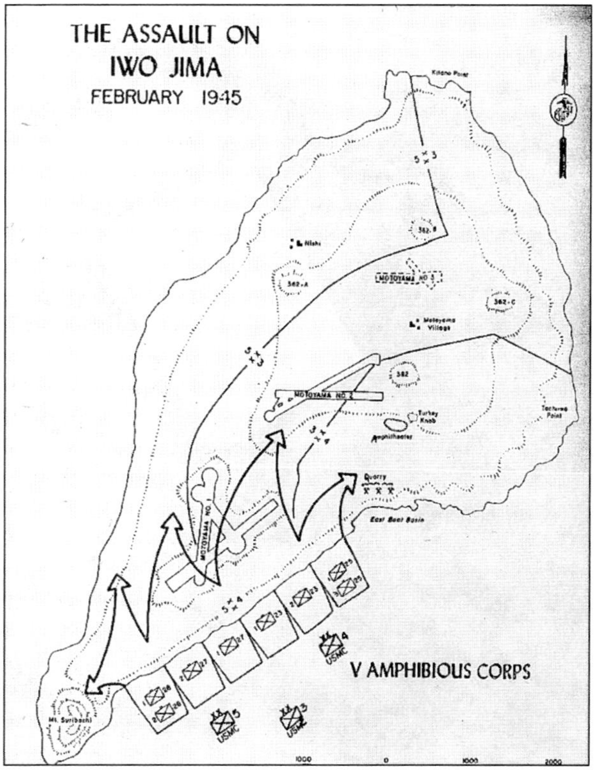

At least two Rutherford County residents participated at Iwo Jima. Navy Lt. J.D. Cooley was Senior Amphibious Beachmaster at the volcanic island. His account of the invasion is titled *Beachmaster at Iwo Jima*; the photo is courtesy of his son Jimmy Dean Cooley.

Assaulting the beaches with the 5th U.S. Marine Division was Company E, 28th Marine Regiment's Pfc. Herman Sims. Capturing Iwo Jima took 36 days and cost the Americans about 6,000 lives with more than 17,000 wounded. Five men in the Marine Division received the Medal of Honor. Sims was unscathed and proud. As a raw rifleman, Sims realized that he and his fellow Marines could become "cannon fodder" during the invasion. During his basic training at Parris Island, South Carolina, Sims's DI (Drill Instructor) had told the raw recruits that they "were worse than the bottom of the barrel; they were from under the barrel." Sims recalls with pride the day of the presentation of the Marine Corps pin. (Courtesy of Herman Sims.)

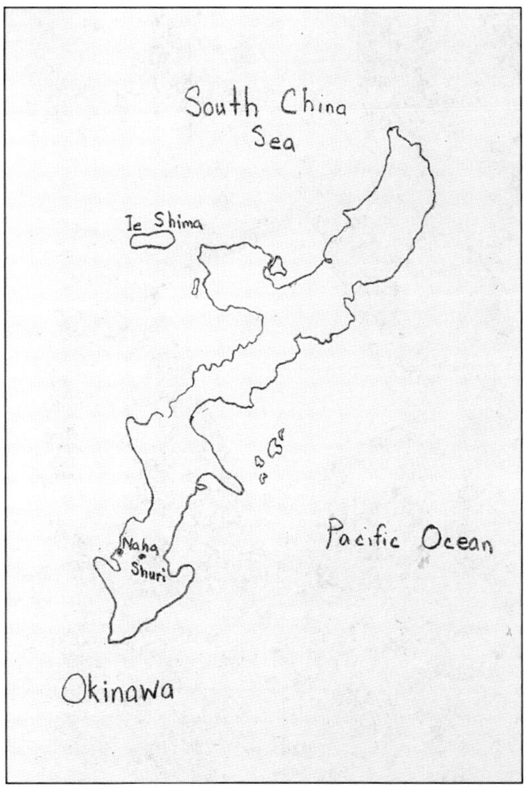


The final island assault of the Pacific War was upon Okinawa. The 60-mile-long island, located 340 miles from the Japanese mainland, was vital to an effective American air campaign against the Japanese Empire. This battle was the most costly battle of the Pacific. On April Fool's Day of 1945, the Third Amphibious Corps (1st U.S. Marine and 6th U.S. Marine Division) and the 24th Army Corps (7th Infantry Division and the 96th Infantry Division) began their assault upon 77,000 Japanese defenders, some of whom were children. American forces made short work of gaining control of the northern two-thirds of the islands. The preponderance of enemy troops were ensconced in the region of Naha and the Shuri Castle. (Courtesy of James M. Walker.)

Pfc. Lawrence Miller Hawkins, 96th Infantry Division, was serving as a litter bearer (stretcher bearer) to help evacuate the numerous American casualties. Hawkins recalls with strong emotion literally having to walk on body parts as they evacuated fellow soldiers and hearing the cries of the wounded mixed with the constant bursts of shell. Private First Class Hawkins suffered severe wounds from a Japanese rocket bomb. He was evacuated to Guam with leg injuries that required eight weeks of hospitalization. (Courtesy of Lawrence Miller Hawkins.)

The Presidential Citation for the Sixth U.S. Marine Division, Reinforced reads in part: "For extraordinary heroism. . .during the assault. . .over the rocky terrain to reduce almost impregnable defenses and capture Sugar Loaf Hill [near] the capital city of Naha." Nineteen-year-old Pvt. Guy Morehead was seriously wounded in the head on May 20, 1945, during the capture of Sugar Loaf Hill. He was hospitalized for 13 weeks at Pearl Harbor. (The information is courtesy of Joy Morehead White.)

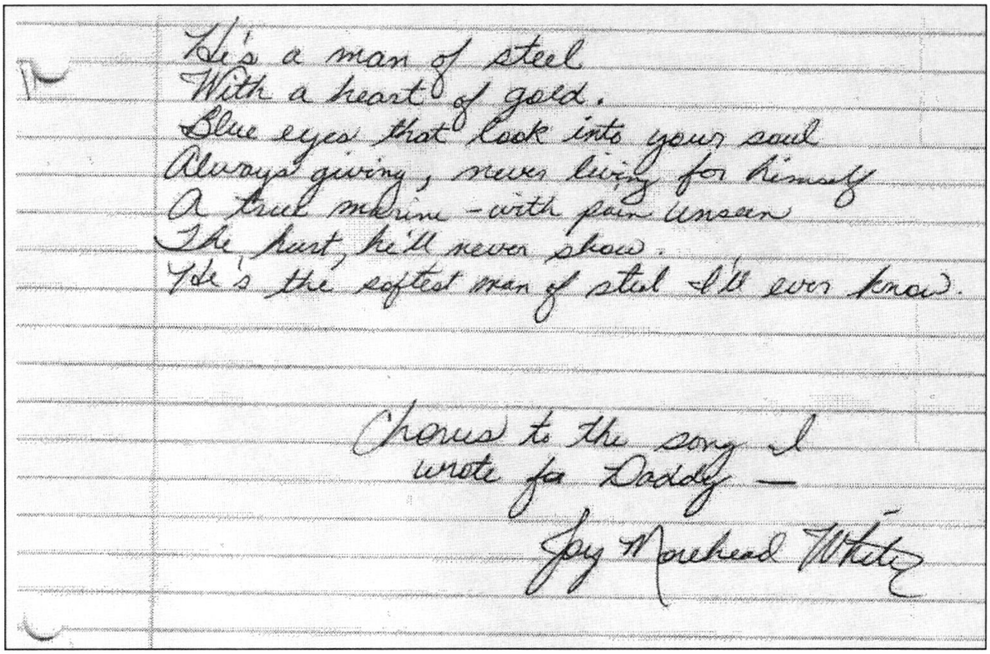

He's a man of steel
With a heart of gold.
Blue eyes that look into your soul
Always giving, never living for himself
A true marine - with pain unseen
The hurt, he'll never show.
He's the softest man of steel I'll ever know.

Chorus to the song I
wrote for Daddy —

Joy Morehead White

Joy Morehead White, daughter of Guy Morehead, wrote a musical tribute to her father. The chorus of "Man of Steel" is used with her permission.

Not as fortunate as Private Morehead, Pvt. Wallace Lonzo Harris fell in combat on Okinawa on June 20, 1945. (Courtesy of Mrs. Johnie B. Harris.)

Private Harris was originally interred in the Sixth Marine Division Cemetery on Okinawa. He was later re-interred in the National Memorial Cemetery of the Pacific, Honolulu, Hawaii. (Courtesy of Mrs. Johnie B. Harris.)

By the middle of August 1945, Okinawa was secure. The B-29s from the United States Army Air Force (specifically the 20th Air Force) had dropped two atomic bombs on Hiroshima and Nagasaki in Japan. By August 14, 1945, Japan surrendered unconditionally. As Pvt. Joe Koon, 7th Infantry Division, walked into his quarters on the night of August 14–15, 1945, a veritable barrage of artillery fire startled him. Minutes later, Koon found out that the Japanese had surrendered. This photograph showing Private Koon (first row, far right) and was taken in Korea after the war; the two men on the back row were interpreters. Koon was part of the occupation troops in Korea. (Courtesy of Joe Koon.)

Vaughn Hamrick was a sailor aboard the USS *Pittsburgh* in 1944–1945. Vaughn, like many Rutherford County servicemen, had a wife (Reba Daves Hamrick). Vaughn had survived action at Iwo Jima and Okinawa. He and Reba were the parents of two children: Bonnie Hamrick (Schultheiss) and Larry Hamrick. The Rutherford County native was not alone at sea. "Bud" McFarland and Eliot James Teseniar, two Rutherford County residents, also sailed on the *Pittsburgh*. (Courtesy of Reba Hamrick.)

Eliot James Teseniar—one of a set of twins—was born on April 4, 1920. Like Vaughn Hamrick, Teseniar survived action at Iwo Jima and Okinawa. Teseniar married Bonnie Mary Dean Rice and they had two daughters. Teseniar later became a Holiness Minister. (Courtesy of Edith Owens.)

Nature posed an unrelenting obstacle to the members of the American fleet. A typhoon struck off Okinawa. On June 4, 1945, the heavy cruiser USS *Pittsburgh* began to fight nature at its worst. By the next day winds had increased to 70 knots (about 75 mph). The 100-foot waves tore at the hull of the ship, buckled the deck, and wrenched the bow free. Vaughn Hamrick sent this postcard home to his wife with the caption: "Rough sailing, huh, honey?" (U.S. Navy postcard and caption courtesy of Reba Hamrick.)

Miraculously the *Pittsburgh* suffered no casualties. The ship slowly steamed to Guam Island for temporary repairs. This photograph shows the USS *Pittsburgh* minus its bow. Alongside the light cruiser is the USS *Duluth*. (Courtesy of Reba Hamrick.)

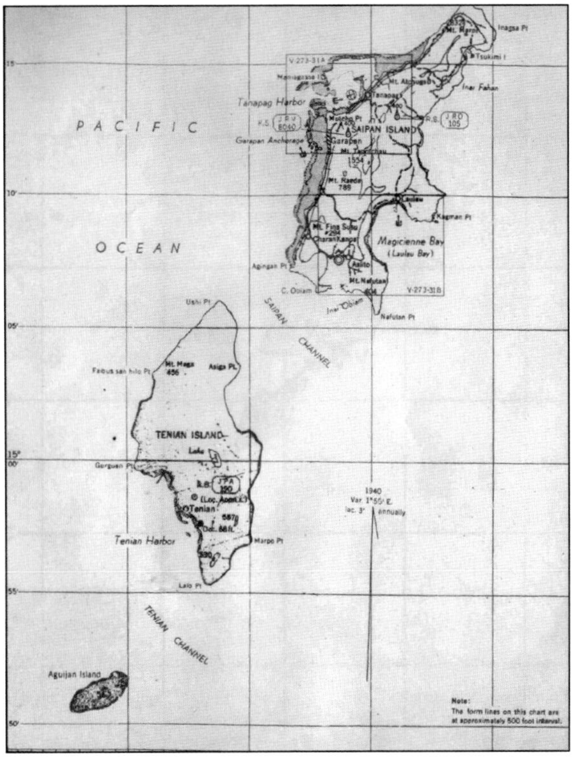


To help force the unconditional surrender of Japan, the United States Air Forces established bases on the captured Central Pacific Islands of Saipan and Tinian. B-29 Superfortress bombers launched the first attack on the Japanese home islands on November 24, 1944. (Courtesy of Gil Mays.)

The United States, with great help from its British allies, had developed the ultimate secret weapon: the atomic bomb. At Oak Ridge, Tennessee, workers used various techniques to separate U235 from U238. Lorene Padgett Hopson, sister to Guy Padgett and wife of Roy E. Hopson, worked at this facility. She was uninformed as to the significance of her duties there. The actual bombs were completed at Los Alamos, New Mexico. (Courtesy of Lorene Padgett Hopson.)

# *Nine*

# JAPAN SURRENDERS (1945)
## ENDING THE WAR

*On August 6, 1945, the United States used the first atomic bomb on the city of Hiroshima. After a second bomb was dropped on Nagasaki on August 9, 1945, Japanese Emperor Hirohito agreed to the terms of unconditional surrender. The signings of the formal documents of surrender were on September 2, 1945, aboard the battleship USS Missouri in Tokyo Harbor.*

Col. Paul Tibbets, piloting the "Enola Gay," the B-29 that he named for his mother, delivered the first atomic bomb (nicknamed "Little Boy") on the city of Hiroshima. The 12.5-kiloton device brought immediate or delayed death to approximately 140,000 people. (Photograph courtesy of Mark Wayne, in memory of his father Rocco Francis Rossi Jr. [Frank Wayne]).

The United States sent armed forces to establish security and to succor the Japanese population. Personnel who witnessed the devastation caused by the atomic bomb were appalled by the destruction but pleased that the war was over. Dwight Green, an American sailor, provided this image of the devastation of a Japanese city. (Courtesy of Dwight Green.)

The leveled city speaks of the atomic bomb's destructive power. This photograph of Hiroshima reminded Dwight Green of the terrible, unforgettable stench wafting from the city as Americans helped with the clean-up. (Courtesy of Dwight Green.)

Even those whose lives and dwellings had been spared bore the mark of sadness, humiliation, and defeat. (Courtesy of Dwight Green.)

At the end of the war, the United States Army assigned dredge crews to clean up Japanese harbors. T-5 Roy E. Hopson of the 4368th Dredge Crew was one of these soldiers. The barge he was on had become disabled, and a Navy ship had taken the soldiers on board—but had not notified the naval authorities. Hopson arrived in Japan on a Navy ship only to find he was listed as "Missing in Action."(Courtesy of Roy E. Hopson.)

Petty Officer Second Class Ralph D. Fisher Jr. served on board the USS *Vesole* (DD 878) in the final days of World War II. The *Vesole* was an escort for supply ships of the Fourth Fleet. These "fleet trains," as they were called, supplied the needs of the task forces that had battered the Japanese into surrender. (Courtesy of Ralph D. Fisher Jr.)

Two of the Lancaster boys, brothers of Mrs. Mary Elizabeth Lancaster Bradley (wife of Willard G. Bradley), served with the United States Army in the Pacific Area of Operations. Fortunately, both (A.B. Lancaster and J.C. Lancaster) returned home to Rutherford County. (Courtesy of Chivous Omar Bradley and Mary Elizabeth Lancaster Bradley.)

# Ten

# THE HOME FRONT (1941–1945)

## DOING OUR PART

*Despite the worsening of the diplomatic situation and the rise of fascism and communism in Europe, America slowly began to recover from the Great Depression. Life went on as usual in most of America.*

One couple began making their plans for the future. Pictured here in 1938 are the parents of James M. Walker, one of the co-authors. The co-author's mother (Nelle Culbreth Walker) and father (James Maze "Dock" Walker) share a moment together on the family farm. (Courtesy of James M. Walker.)

A staple of pre-War Army life was sports competition. Serving in Panama was Falls W. Price. Price was a middle-weight champion boxer for his unit. Falls attributes his quick hands to picking cotton on the farm. (Courtesy of Falls W. Price.)

War came to Europe in September 1939. Germany rapidly defeated Poland and France. The United Kingdom stood defiantly in Hitler's way. Under the charismatic and dynamic leadership of Prime Minister Winston Churchill, England continued to hold its head high in the face of the Nazi onslaught. President Roosevelt, in an attempt to keep the United Kingdom in the war, authorized neutrality patrols in the North Atlantic. On October 17, 1941, a German U-Boat torpedoed the USS *Kearny*. Eleven men were lost. Surviving the attack was Firecontrol Chief Petty Officer James Allen Adams Jr. (Courtesy of Mrs. Emily M. Adams.)

While the war raged in Europe and tensions mounted in the Pacific, life went on as usual for much of small-town America. On the afternoon of December 7, 1941, the Woodmen of the World gathered for a photograph on the stone bleachers of Ellenboro School. When the families arrived home, they found that Japan had bombed Pearl Harbor. Reid and Meredith Bedford are holding their son Jerrell (third row from the top, seventh from the left). Zeb Daves, who later served in the Pacific, is the last one on the right end of the second row. (Courtesy of Jerrell Bedford.)

The American people united behind their leader, Franklin Delano Roosevelt. After Congress declared war on Monday, December 8, 1941, the nation rapidly mobilized for the tremendous task ahead. Before the end of the war about 5,000 people from Rutherford County would serve their nation in the armed forces. Many people hung President Roosevelt's picture with that of family members on their mantles and walls. This plaque from the 1940s is from the collection of Anita Price Davis.

Not only men but women, too, served their country. Sunshine Tedder trained as a nurse to help in war time. Sara Jolley remembers women gathering on the top floor of the R.R. Haynes Memorial Building in Cliffside to roll bandages. Here on the far left Martha McCrary (Price), a WAVE (Women Accepted for Volunteer Emergency Service), is pictured near her station at Elizabeth City, North Carolina. (Courtesy of Falls W. Price.)

A.B. Bushong was the Ellenboro Air Raid Warden for the Office of Civil Defense. The highest point in Ellenboro was near Elijah Hamrick's residence. Mr. Hamrick's daughter Evelyn ("Polly") Hamrick (later wife of Ivey Ray Mauney) often made the morning call to report an all-clear. The code words were "Bacon 28." A.B. Bushong's daughter Helen remembers making calls from Ellenboro to Headquarters. A typical call might be "Bacon 28 reporting. Sighted 3 planes, flying low, two engines, flying east from the north." This was during the daytime, of course. Nighttime was more serene with the blackouts.(Courtesy of Evelyn ["Polly"] Hamrick Mauney.)

With men away in training and in critical war industries, women assumed new roles and increased responsibilities for the family. Here Mary Elizabeth Lancaster (Bradley), wife of Willard G. Bradley, is pictured picking cotton. (Courtesy of Chivous Omar Bradley.)

County boys and men responded to their nation's call. These men were trained for all branches of service all over the United States, from Ft. Bragg, North Carolina, to Camp Wolter, Texas, to San Luis Obispo, California, and to many other locations. County resident Ray Pegram received his training in Kansas City, Missouri. Pegram is the third man on the right of the "V" in the back row. (Courtesy of Ray Pegram.)

Clustered around a 1929 Model "A" Ford are six pre-war friends. They are, from left to right, (front row) Walter Powell, George Whitaker, and Timer Tessneer; (back row) Iven Bridges (KIA on Leyte Island on December 14, 1944), Hal Bridges, and R.C. Tessneer (KIA during the invasion of Saipan Island). (Courtesy of Ronnie Powell.)

(*below, left*) Many men from Rutherford County served. Our incomplete information makes retelling their stories impossible, another reason for preserving what we do know now. Sgt. Virgil L. Blanton served with Company A, 311th Infantry Regiment. Blanton received the CIB (Combat Infantryman's Badge) for his distinguished service in combat. Blanton was in the European Theater of Operations Advanced Base. He helped provide service and supplies for all Army units. (Courtesy of Bertha Lancaster Gallman, Junie Mason Blanton, Donald R. Blanton, and Martha R. Blanton; it was delivered by Edith Owens.)

(*below, right*) Sgt. John Frank Walker Jr. served in the Pacific Theater. He was a member of an anti-tank battalion, United States Army. (Courtesy of Diane Jones.)

James Maze ("Dock") Walker served his nation by working at the United States Rubber Company, Charlotte plant. Too old for conscription, Walker contributed to the war effort by delivering 40-mm shells to testing sites at Memphis, Tennessee, and Dahlgren, Virginia. (Courtesy of James M. Walker.)

W. Henry Edwards, United States Coast Guard, served stateside from 1942 (when he volunteered) throughout the war. Edwards's original duty was that of a shoreman based at Ocean City, Maryland. Edwards and his fellow "coastees" patrolled the Atlantic beaches. At night they used wheeled vehicles, but by day the men rode ponies. Edwards remembers the beauty of looking back as they rode and seeing the tide erase their tracks. (Notice the half-shields on the headlights for Civil Defense purposes.) (Courtesy of W. Henry Edwards.)

Not satisfied with his duty, Edwards requested active ship duty and was assigned to the USS *Grand Island* (PF 14) as a signalman. The *Grand Island* acted as a navigator ship and escorted ships to Alamida, California. (Courtesy of W. Henry Edwards.)

Furloughs were bittersweet times because the families often thought of where their loved one might be deployed. Here James Avery Morehead (brother of Guy Morehead) spends a few treasured minutes with a young family member. Morehead was certain his next assignment would be "somewhere overseas," but a medical discharge brought him back home from California to continue his job at Grindstaff's Furniture. (Courtesy of Aileen Morehead.)

Leroy Nolan, Water Tender 2nd Class on board USS *Fogg* (DE 47), was at sea when Germany surrendered. Nolan recalls his wonderful celebration with the other sailors. The *Fogg* had been escorting convoys in the North Atlantic. Nolan said, "The first time I ever saw the ocean was from the side of a ship." (Courtesy of Leroy Nolan.) No photograph was available of Corp. Raymond H. Bailey, who served the United States Army Air Forces on the island of Bermuda. His duty was to check with the pilot about supplies needed to continue their supply-flights to Europe or to America with wounded troops. Bailey recalled one special flight that was transporting "crates of gold bullion" to France.

Serving with the 389the G/S Engineers was William E. Peeler. Peeler served in England, France, Belgium, and Germany. Peeler was trained to use a .50-caliber machine gun; he recalls building bridges to facilitate the Allied advances. (Courtesy of William E. Peeler.)

Pfc. Walter Gaines Adair served in Company A, the 289th Infantry regiment. Adair received the Combat Infantryman's Badge and a Bronze Star for his services in the campaign in Germany in 1945. His brothers Albert Lee Adair and Sam Adair also distinguished themselves in their service. (Photographs courtesy of Genell Harris Adair and were delivered by Mrs. Edith Owens.) Fred Paul Matheny (no photograph available) attests to the harshness of war. He was a member of the Horse Cavalry. His duty for a while was in a hospital near Oklahoma City; there he personally saw the casualties of war. Matheny also knew personal loss; his brother Clyde Marvin Matheny made the supreme sacrifice.

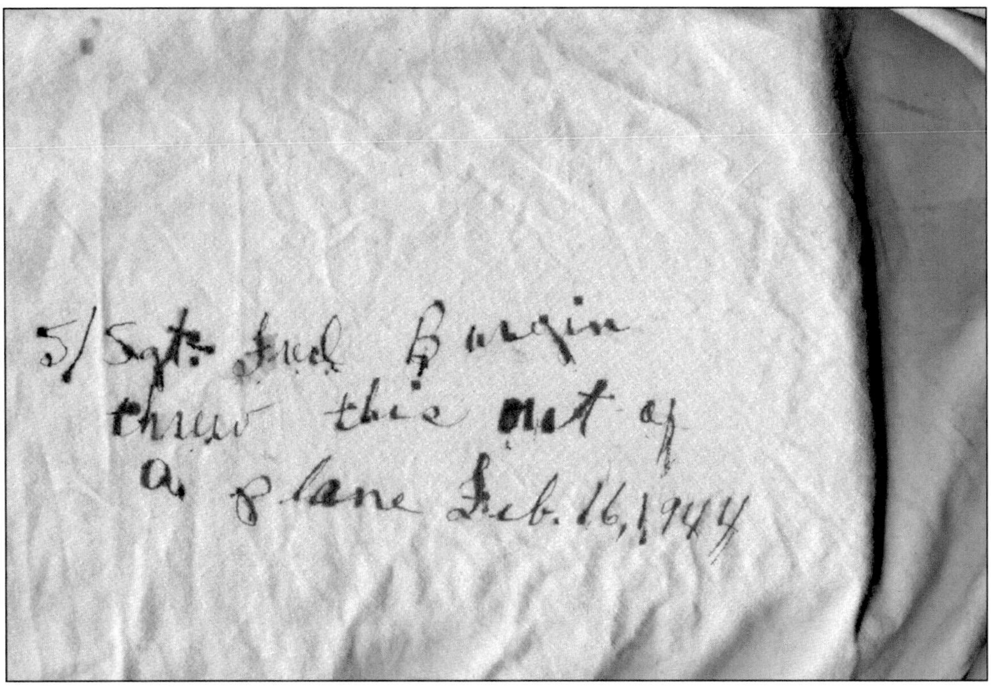


Tech Sgt. Fred Burgin of the 450th Bomb Group was one of four brothers who entered service during World War II. On a flight that passed near Forest City, Burgin asked the pilot to "buzz" his home. Grabbing some mechanics' rags, pieces of metal for weight, and string, Burgin dropped a "parachute" at his home; his mother kept it. (Courtesy of Fred Burgin.)

Burgin's plane was shot down on a bombing mission over Austria on March 19, 1944. His first parachute jump was from the plane. On his way down, he saw the pilot of the enemy aircraft wave at him from the cockpit; Burgin waved back and was surprised that the pilot did not shoot at him. Burgin talks of marching for months with just the clothes on his back and drying his socks each night in his arm pits. He was in the same POW camp as Guy Padgett. (Courtesy of Fred Burgin.)

In 1944–1945, an explosion destroyed a convoy approaching Puzzle Creek near Forest City. Residents miles away heard the noise. Here Blaine B. Logan Sr. (with hat) looks at the twisted remains. The cause of the explosion has remained a mystery. Area residents whispered sabotage, but there was no repeat. The incident is known throughout the county as "The Battle of Puzzle Creek." (Courtesy of Blaine B. Logan Jr.)

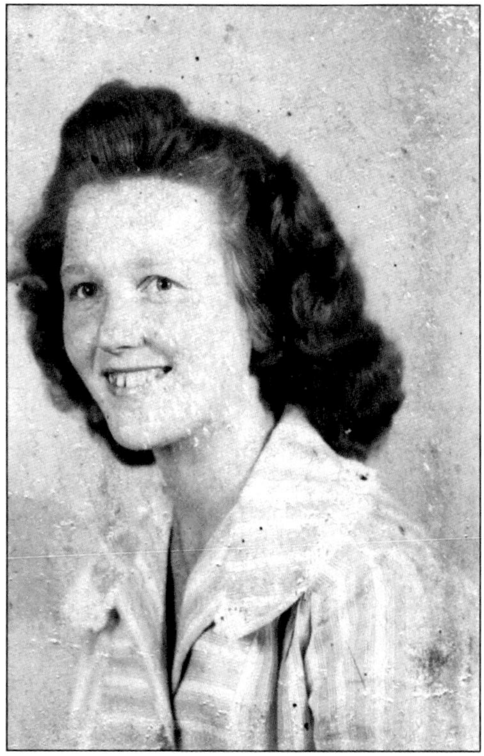

Armond L. Whitener served on board the USS *Decker*. When he was in port in New York City, his wife Callie Waters Whitener (Wright) was able to leave her job as a telephone operator to visit him. She recollects "listening to the people talking, the fast driving, and the people shouting," breakfast that included hash browns and no biscuits, and visiting one of the great Cunard Line Passenger "Queens" that had been transporting soldiers across the Atlantic. (Photos courtesy of Callie Waters Whitener Wright.)

Edith Owens found this photograph in the home she purchased in 1961. Although she did not know the person, she could not throw away his image. Just as the United States honors the unknown with the Tomb of the Unknown Soldiers, *Rutherford County in World War II* pays tribute to all who served. (Courtesy of Edith Owens.)

The end of World War II brought many changes. Such was the case for Leon and Winifred McDaniel. Married in England, "Winnie" McDaniel came to the United States on the S.L. *Washington* after the end of the war. More than half a century later, the couple still resides in Ellenboro. (Wedding photograph courtesy of Leon and Winifred McDaniel.)

The long-awaited homecomings of service personnel were memorable. When 11-year-old Polly Smith's brother Floyd (United States Army Air Forces) was due to return home, she waited all day at the bus stop in Alexander for him. When Floyd (seated) at last arrived, he scooped both Polly and her friend up in his arms and carried them both all the way home. Palmer (standing) also served his country well in the United States Army Combat Engineers. (Courtesy of Polly Smith Nolan.)

There was much celebration at the end of the war. For some, however, the end was bittersweet because our county had more than its share of casualties. Although all those who served are heroes and must be remembered, those who made the supreme sacrifice must not be forgotten. *REAL HEROES: Rutherford County Men Who Made the Supreme Sacrifice During World War II* contains numerous photographs and a brief biographical sketch of each of the 148 county men who made the supreme sacrifice.

Pictured here is the homecoming of Pfc. Marvin D. Morrow of the First Army. The Honor Guard surrounds the first Rutherford County World War II service man returned from overseas for burial. Members of the American Legion of the Willis Towery Post bear his flag-draped coffin. (Courtesy of Clarence Morrow, Marvin's brother.)